HERE COMES
spring

FRESH AND FUN QUILTED
PROJECTS FOR YOUR HOME

Jeanne Large and Shelley Wicks

Martingale®
Create with Confidence

Here Comes Spring:
Fresh and Fun Quilted Projects for Your Home
© 2016 by Jeanne Large and Shelley Wicks

Martingale®
19021 120th Ave. NE, Ste. 102
Bothell, WA 98011-9511 USA
ShopMartingale.com

Printed in China
21 20 19 18 17 16   8 7 6 5 4 3 2 1

Library of Congress Cataloging-in-Publication Data
is available upon request.

ISBN: 978-1-60468-723-1

MISSION STATEMENT

Dedicated to providing quality products
and service to inspire creativity.

CREDITS

PUBLISHER AND
CHIEF VISIONARY OFFICER
Jennifer Erbe Keltner

CONTENT DIRECTOR
Karen Costello Soltys

DESIGN MANAGER
Adrienne Smitke

MANAGING EDITOR
Tina Cook

PRODUCTION MANAGER
Regina Girard

ACQUISITIONS EDITOR
Karen M. Burns

PHOTOGRAPHER
Brent Kane

TECHNICAL EDITOR
Ellen Pahl

ILLUSTRATOR
Rose Wright

COPY EDITOR
Durby Peterson

SPECIAL THANKS
*Thanks to Cliff and Rosemary Bailey of Snohomish,
Washington, for allowing the photography for this
book to take place in their home.*

Contents

Introduction   5

Opening Day Trio   6
    Opening Day Lap Quilt   6
    Opening Day Table Runner   10
    Opening Day Pillow   13

Rebecca's Keepsake Quilt   18

Time-Out Lap Quilt   27

My Heart Is in the Garden   33

Plum Pretty Collection   40
    Plum Pretty Lap Quilt   40
    Plum Pretty Doll Quilt   44
    Plum Pretty Doll Tote   46

Ziggy Quilt   50

Country Cottage Bed Quilt   57

Prairie Picnic Set   62
    Prairie Picnic Quilt   62
    Prairie Picnic Tote   69

Spring Blooms Duo   75
    Spring Blooms Wall Hanging   75
    Spring Blooms Table Topper   81

Quiltmaking Techniques   92

About the Authors   96

Bonus Patterns online!
Visit ShopMartingale.com/extras to download "Rebecca's Table Runner" and "Bella Blossoms Lap Quilt" for free.

- Strawberries $2/lb
- Lettuce $2/head
- Swiss chard + kale $2/lb
- snap peas $3/

Introduction

Spring is in the air! *There's nowhere that the coming of spring means so much as on the Canadian Prairies. Our winters can be long and cold, so the promise of spring is truly something to celebrate. You can sense that people feel lighter. They smile more, they wave to their neighbors, and you actually see more people outside, walking and enjoying the outdoors. It's a time to throw back the curtains, fling open the windows, and let that spring air flow through your home!*

For those of us who decorate with quilts, it's time to change things up. Put those snowmen quilts away and bring out the flowers! It's amazing how you can change the look of a room by adding or changing a quilt. Try our "Spring Blooms Wall Hanging" in an entryway or on the front porch—it'll be a great welcome to your home, and it certainly adds a fresh seasonal feeling to a room.

The projects in this book are designed to inspire you and rejuvenate your enthusiasm for quilting. Whether you make one of these quilts in colors similar to ours or in hues to suit your home decor, we know you'll enjoy the journey from winter to spring.

~ Jeanne and Shelley

Opening Day Trio

> Welcome spring with this simple yet striking quilt. The cheery yellow flowers will brighten any room in your house! To usher the season into your home in a big way, make the coordinating pillow and runner.

Opening Day Lap Quilt

Designed by Jeanne Large and Shelley Wicks; machine quilted by Wendy Findlay

FINISHED QUILT: 55½" x 63½"

MATERIALS

Yardage is based on 42"-wide fabric. Fat eighths measure approximately 9" x 21".

1 yard of black tone on tone #1 for inner border and binding

½ yard of black tone on tone #2 for checkerboard

1 fat eighth of black tone on tone #3 for flower centers

⅔ yard of red tone on tone #1 for outer border

⅝ yard *each* of 3 red tone on tones #2 for appliqué backgrounds and blocks

¼ yard *each* of 3 red tone on tones #3 for blocks

½ yard of off-white fabric for checkerboard

12" x 14" piece *each* of 3 yellow prints for flowers

1 fat eighth of green tone on tone for leaves

3⅝ yards of fabric for backing

64" x 72" piece of batting

2¾ yards of ⅝"-wide green rickrack for stems

1½ yards of 18"-wide lightweight fusible web

Matching thread and dark-charcoal thread for appliqué

CUTTING

Cut all strips across the width of the fabric.

From *each* of the red tone on tones #2, cut:
1 strip, 9½" x 42"; crosscut into 2 rectangles, 9½" x 16½" (6 total)
1 strip, 6½" x 42"; crosscut into 5 squares, 6½" x 6½" (15 total)

From *each* of the red tone on tones #3, cut:
1 strip, 6½" x 42"; crosscut into 5 squares, 6½" x 6½" (15 total)

From the black tone on tone #2, cut:
4 strips, 3½" x 42"

From the off-white fabric, cut:
4 strips, 3½" x 42"

From the black tone on tone #1, cut:
6 strips, 2" x 42"
7 strips, 2½" x 42"

From the red tone on tone #1, cut:
6 strips, 3½" x 42"

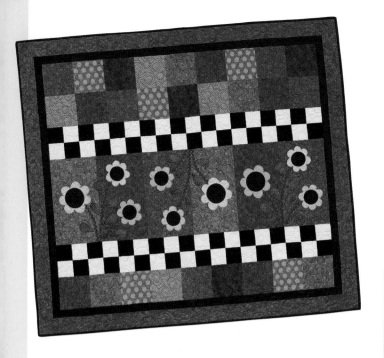

PIECING

1. Arrange 27 of the red 6½" squares into three rows of nine squares each. (You'll have three extra squares.) Sew the squares together to make three long rows. Press the seam allowances in opposite directions from row to row. Sew two of the rows together. Press the seam allowances to one side.

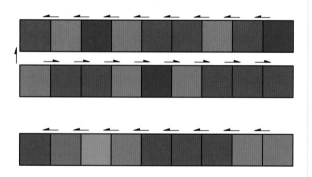

2. Sew a black 3½" strip to the long edge of an off-white 3½" strip to make a strip set. Press the seam allowances toward the black strip. Make four strip sets. Crosscut each strip set into nine 3½" segments for a total of 36.

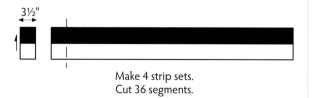

3½"

Make 4 strip sets.
Cut 36 segments.

3. Sew 18 of the segments together, alternating them to make a checkerboard row. Press the seam allowances to one side. Make two long checkerboard rows.

Make 2.

4. Sew a checkerboard row to one side of each of the red units from step 1 as shown. Press the seam allowances toward the red units.

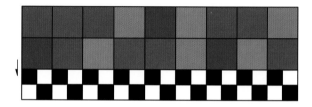

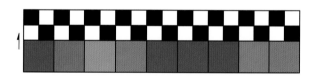

5. Sew two red 9½" x 16½" rectangles together along the long edges. Press the seam allowances to one side. Make three rectangle units.

Make 3.

APPLIQUÉ

1. Referring to "Fusible-Web Appliqué" on page 92, use the patterns on pages 15 and 16 to prepare the following:

   - 2 small flowers from each yellow print (6 total)
   - 1 large flower from each yellow print (3 total)
   - 6 small flower centers from black tone on tone #3
   - 3 large flower centers from black tone on tone #3
   - 18 leaves from green tone on tone

2. Referring to "Using Rickrack" on page 95 and the appliqué placement diagram below, position, trim, and pin the rickrack stems in place on a red rectangle unit. Select two small flowers and one large flower (each flower from a different yellow print) and six leaves. Arrange the prepared appliqué shapes on the background and fuse in place, being careful not to scorch the rickrack. Use matching thread to sew a straight line down the center of each rickrack stem. Use dark-charcoal thread to blanket-stitch around each shape by hand or machine. Repeat to make a total of three blocks.

Make 3.

ASSEMBLING THE QUILT TOP

1. Sew together the three red appliqué blocks as shown. Press the seam allowances in one direction.

2. Arrange the three sections of the quilt as shown and sew them together. Press the seam allowances toward the appliqué panel.

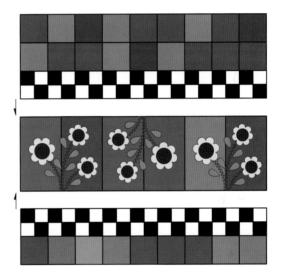

3. Sew the black 2" x 42" strips end to end to create one long continuous strip. From this, cut two strips, 2" x 54½", and two strips, 2" x 49½". Sew the 54½"-long strips to the sides of the quilt. Sew the 49½"-long strips to the top and bottom of the quilt. Press the seam allowances toward the black border.

4. Sew the red 3½" x strips end to end to create one long continuous strip. From this, cut two strips, 3½" x 57½", and two strips, 3½" x 55½". Sew the 57½"-long strips to the sides of the quilt. Sew the 55½"-long strips to the top and bottom of the quilt. Press the seam allowances toward the red border.

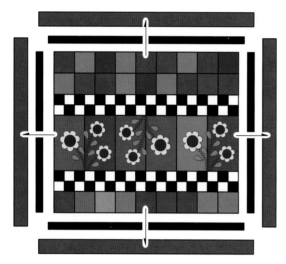

Quilt assembly

FINISHING THE QUILT

For help with any of the following steps, visit ShopMartingale.com/extras to get free, downloadable instructions.

1. Layer the backing, batting, and quilt top; baste.

2. Quilt as desired. Ours is machine quilted with an allover design.

3. Bind the quilt using the remaining black 2½"-wide strips.

Opening Day Table Runner

Designed by Jeanne Large and Shelley Wicks; machine quilted by Jeanne Large

FINISHED RUNNER: 13" x 41"

MATERIALS

Yardage is based on 42"-wide fabric. Fat eighths measure approximately 9" x 21".

1½ yards of black print for background
1⅓ yards of red print for runner center and backing
1 fat eighth of dark-yellow polka dot for flowers
6" x 18" piece of black solid for flower centers
5" x 11" piece of gold check for stars
18" x 50" piece of batting
3⅞ yards of ⅝"-wide black rickrack
1⅔ yards of ½"-wide green rickrack
½ yard of 18"-wide lightweight fusible web
Matching thread for appliqué
8 green buttons, 1" diameter, for tongues
Lightweight cardboard or other template material

CUTTING

From the black print, cut *on the lengthwise grain*:
1 piece, 18" x 50"

From the red print, cut *on the lengthwise grain*:
1 rectangle, 13½" x 41½"
2 rectangles, 8½" x 30½"

From the remainder of the red print, cut:
16 rectangles, 2½" x 4"

MAKING THE BACKGROUND

1. Layer the black 18" x 50" rectangle on top of the batting and quilt in an allover design. Trim to measure 13½" x 41½".

2. Using the pattern on page 17, make a cutting guide from lightweight cardboard. Place the guide on a corner, mark the curve, and trim to make the rounded ends. Repeat on each corner.

Trim.

3. Referring to "Using Rickrack" on page 95, pin the black rickrack along the outer edge, with one edge of the bumps directly along the fabric edge. Sew all around using ¼" seam allowance.

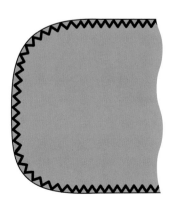

4. Use the cutting guide to trim the corners of the red 13½" x 41½" rectangle as you did the black background.

5. Place the trimmed red piece on the quilted black background, right sides together. Match the outer edges and pin all around. Sew around the outer edge directly over the previous line of stitching, leaving a 6" opening along one side.

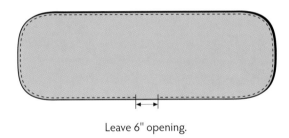

Leave 6" opening.

6. Turn right side out and press. Hand stitch the opening closed.

APPLIQUÉ

1. Referring to "Fusible-Web Appliqué" on page 92, use the patterns on page 16 to prepare the following:

   ◆ 3 large flowers from dark-yellow polka dot

   ◆ 7 stars from gold check

2. Referring to "Using Rickrack as an Edging" on page 95, prepare three large flower centers using black fabric, the green rickrack, and the pattern on page 16.

3. Using the diagram below as a guide, arrange the three flowers and four of the stars on one of the red 8½" x 30½" rectangles. Fuse the shapes in place and appliqué by hand or machine. Pin the flower centers in place and sew them down along the edge of the rickrack using matching thread. Fuse and appliqué the remaining three stars on the flower centers.

FINISHING THE RUNNER

1. Make a template for the tongue using the pattern on page 17. Trace around the template onto the wrong side of eight of the red 2½" x 4" rectangles, with the straight edge along one 2½" edge.

2. Layer each traced rectangle with a plain red 2½" x 4" rectangle, right sides together. Sew directly on the drawn line, leaving the straight edge open. Trim all around ¹⁄₁₆" outside the stitching line. Turn right side out and press. Make eight tongues.

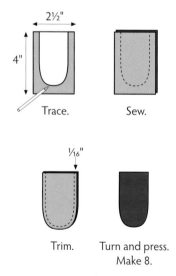

2½"

4"

Trace.   Sew.

¹⁄₁₆"

Trim.   Turn and press.
          Make 8.

3. With the runner right side up, and using the diagram as a guide, lay four tongues across one end, raw edges even. The tongues on the outer edges should be ¼" from the side of the runner to allow for the seam. Pin in place. Repeat on the opposite end of the runner. Sew across each end ⅛" in from the edge to secure the tongues.

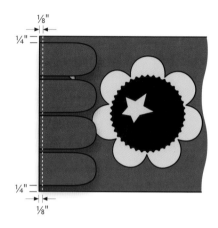

⅛"
¼"

¼"
⅛"

4. Place the remaining red 8½" x 30½" rectangle over the appliquéd section, right sides together. Pin in place and sew around the outside edges using ¼" seam allowance and leaving a 6" opening along one side. Turn right side out and press flat. Hand stitch the opening closed.

5. Position the runner on top of the black background, measuring all around to be sure it's centered. Pin in place and topstitch all around the red rectangle, ¹⁄₁₆" from the outer edges. Do not sew around the tongues; they should remain loose.

6. Sew a green button on each tongue to secure it in place.

Opening Day Pillow

Designed by Jeanne Large and Shelley Wicks; machine quilted by Jeanne Large

FINISHED PILLOW: 14½" x 22½"

MATERIALS

Yardage is based on 42"-wide fabric. Fat quarters measure approximately 18" x 21".

⅞ yard of black print for checkerboard, border, and backing

1 fat quarter of red tone on tone for pillow center

⅛ yard of white tone on tone for checkerboard

6" x 6" piece *each* of 3 assorted yellow prints for flowers

8" x 8" piece of green print for leaves

4" x 12" piece of black solid for flower centers

2 pieces of batting, 20" x 30"

1⅛ yards of ½"-wide green rickrack

½ yard of 18"-wide lightweight fusible web

Dark-charcoal thread for appliqué

16 ounces of fiberfill

CUTTING

Cut all strips across the width of the fabric.

From the white tone on tone, cut:
1 strip, 2" x 42"

From the black print, cut:
1 strip, 2" x 42"
2 strips, 2½" x 42"; crosscut into:
    2 pieces, 2½" x 19"
    2 pieces, 2½" x 15"
1 piece, 18" x 26"

From the red tone on tone, cut:
1 piece, 11" x 13"

PIECING

1. Sew the white 2" x 42" strip and the black 2" x 42" strip together along the long edges to make a strip set. Press the seam allowances toward the black strip. Crosscut into 14 segments, 2" wide.

Cut 14 segments.

2. Sew seven of the segments together, rotating them to make a checkerboard. Make two checkerboard sections.

Make 2.

3. Sew one checkerboard section to each 11" edge of the red 11" x 13" piece. Press the seam allowances toward the red piece.

4. Sew a black 2½" x 19" piece to each side of the pillow center. Press the seam allowances toward the black border. Sew the black 2½" x 15" pieces to the top and bottom. Press.

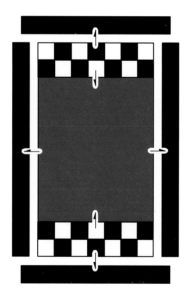

Pillow assembly

5. Place the pillow top right side up on one of the 20" x 30" pieces of batting. Stitch in the ditch along the border seamlines and along the vertical lines of the checkerboard. Trim the batting even with the edge of the pillow top.

6. Place the black 18" x 26" piece right side up on the remaining 20" x 30" piece of batting. Quilt using an allover design. Trim to measure 15" x 23".

APPLIQUÉ

1. Referring to "Fusible-Web Appliqué" on page 92, use the patterns on pages 15 and 16 to prepare the following:

   ♦ 3 small flowers from assorted yellow prints
   ♦ 3 small flowers centers from black solid
   ♦ 6 leaves from green print

2. Referring to "Using Rickrack" on page 95, and the appliqué placement diagram below, pin the rickrack stems in place on the pillow top. Arrange the prepared appliqué shapes and press in place, being careful not to scorch the rickrack. Use matching thread to sew a straight line down the center of each rickrack stem. Use dark-charcoal thread to blanket-stitch around each shape by hand or machine.

FINISHING THE PILLOW

1. Lay the pillow front and back right sides together with raw edges even; pin in place. Sew all around, using ¼" seam allowance and leaving a 6" opening along one side. Trim the corner seam allowances diagonally and turn right side out. Press.

2. Stuff the pillow through the opening and then stitch the opening closed by hand.

Patterns are reversed for fusible appliqué.

Small flower
Make 6 for lap quilt.
Make 3 for pillow.

Small flower center
Make 6 for lap quilt.
Make 3 for pillow.

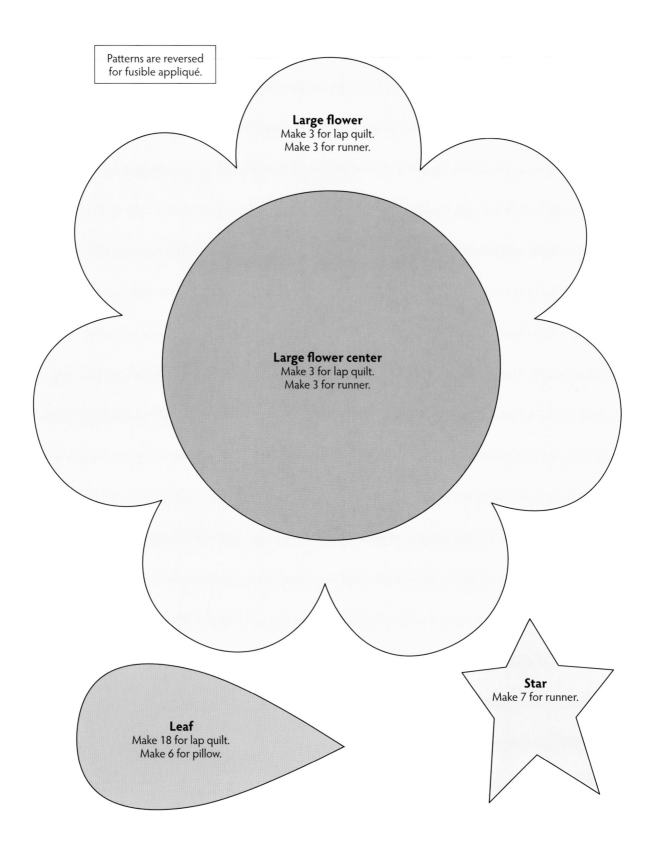

Patterns are reversed for fusible appliqué.

Large flower
Make 3 for lap quilt.
Make 3 for runner.

Large flower center
Make 3 for lap quilt.
Make 3 for runner.

Leaf
Make 18 for lap quilt.
Make 6 for pillow.

Star
Make 7 for runner.

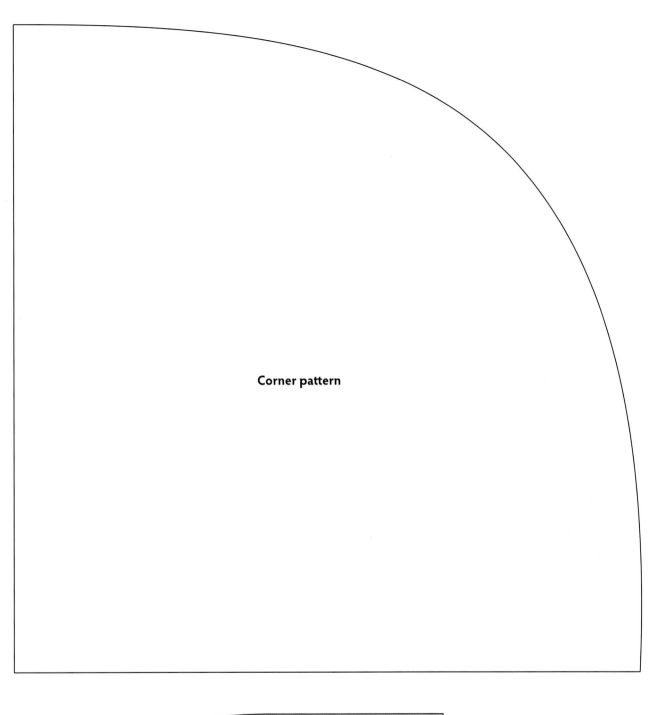

Corner pattern

Tongue
Trace 8 for runner.

Rebecca's Keepsake Quilt

> We designed this quilt for Rebecca, as a keepsake to help her remember her three years on the Canadian Prairies. She stepped into our hearts with her first visit to our store and quickly became a good friend and valued employee. She returned to England with a wonderful love of quilting!

Designed by Jeanne Large and Shelley Wicks; machine quilted by Wendy Findlay

FINISHED QUILT: 76½" x 88½"

MATERIALS

Yardage is based on 42"-wide fabric. Fat quarters measure approximately 18" x 21". Fat eighths are approximately 9" x 21".

6½ yards of light-beige tone on tone for block backgrounds and border

6 fat quarters *each* of assorted red and gold prints for stars and appliqué

1⅓ yards of red print for inner border and binding

4 fat quarters of assorted green prints for stars and appliqué

7 fat eighths of assorted brown prints for basket appliqué

5½ yards of fabric for backing

85" x 97" piece of batting

5⅔ yards of ½"-wide green rickrack

4¼ yards of 18"-wide lightweight fusible web

Dark-brown thread for appliqué

CUTTING

Cut all strips across the width of fabric.

From *each* of the red, gold, and green fat quarters, cut:

1 strip, 3½" x 21"; crosscut into 5 squares, 3½" x 3½" (80 total)

1 strip, 4½" x 21"; crosscut into 1 square, 4½" x 4½" (16 total); trim the remaining strip to 3½" wide and crosscut into 3 squares, 3½" x 3½" (48 total)

From the light-beige tone on tone, cut:

7 strips, 12½" x 42"; crosscut into 7 rectangles, 12½" x 24½"

16 strips, 4½" x 42"; crosscut into 128 squares, 4½" x 4½"

8 strips, 6½" x 42"

From the red yardage, cut:

16 strips, 2½" x 42"

PIECING

1. Using a pencil and ruler, lightly draw a diagonal line from corner to corner on the wrong side of each red, gold, and green 3½" square.

2. Layer a marked square on one corner of a beige 4½" square with right sides together as shown. Sew from corner to corner directly on the drawn line. Fold the corner back and align it with the corner of the square beneath it; press. Trim away excess layers of fabric beneath the triangle, leaving ¼" seam allowance. Repeat on the adjacent corner with a matching 3½" square. Make four matching star-point units.

Make 4.

3. Sew two of the star-point units to the sides of the matching 4½" square. Press the seam allowances toward the center square.

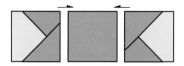

4. Sew a beige 4½" square to each end of the remaining two matching star-point units. Press the seam allowances toward the beige squares. Sew the star-point units to the top and bottom of the center unit. Press the seam allowances toward the center.

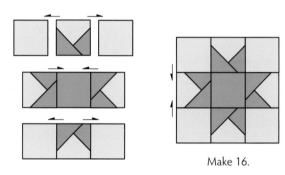

Make 16.

5. Repeat steps 2–4 to make 16 Star blocks.

APPLIQUÉ

1. Referring to "Fusible-Web Appliqué" on page 92, use the patterns on pages 22–26 to prepare the following:

   ♦ 1 basket, basket handle, and basket rim from *each* brown fat eighth (7 total)

   ♦ 7 each of leaf A, B, and C from remaining green prints

   ♦ 7 of flower center C from remaining green prints

   ♦ 14 of flower base D from remaining green prints

   ♦ 7 of flower A from remaining red prints

   ♦ 7 of flower C from remaining red prints

   ♦ 14 of flower D from remaining red prints

   ♦ 7 stars from remaining gold prints

- 7 of flower center A from remaining gold prints
- 7 of flower B from remaining gold prints
- 7 of flower center B from remaining gold prints
- 14 of flower center D from remaining gold prints

2. Using the diagram below and the photo on page 20 as a guide, arrange a basket and matching handle on a 12½" x 24½" background rectangle; fuse in place. Leave the basket rim off until you've fused and stitched the flowers and stems.

3. Arrange the flower and leaf appliqué shapes and cut the rickrack stems. Fuse the appliqués in place. Referring to "Using Rickrack" on page 95, sew the stems down with matching thread.

4. Add a contrasting basket rim and star. Fuse in place. Stitch around each shape using dark-brown thread and blanket-stitch either by hand or machine.

Make 7.

ASSEMBLING THE QUILT TOP

1. Lay out the blocks as shown below, alternating the Star blocks and Flower Basket blocks. Sew the Star blocks together in pairs, and press the seam allowances to one side.

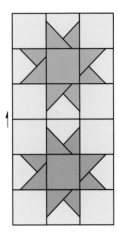

2. Sew the blocks together into three rows. Press the seam allowances toward the Flower Basket blocks. Sew the rows together. Press the seam allowances to one side.

Quilt assembly

3. Sew seven of the red 2½" x 42" strips end to end to create one long continuous strip. From this, cut two strips, 2½" x 72½", and two strips, 2½" x 64½". Sew the 72½"-long strips to the sides of the quilt. Sew the 64½"-long strips to the top and bottom of the quilt. Press the seam allowances toward the red border.

4. Sew the light-beige 6½" x 42" strips end to end to create one long continuous strip. From this, cut four strips, 6½" x 76½". Sew two strips to the sides of the quilt. Sew the remaining two strips to the top and bottom of the quilt. Press the seam allowances toward the red border.

FINISHING THE QUILT

For help with any of the following steps, visit ShopMartingale.com/extras to get free, downloadable instructions.

1. Layer the backing, batting, and quilt top; baste.

2. Quilt as desired. Ours is quilted in an allover design.

3. Bind the quilt using the remaining red 2½"-wide strips.

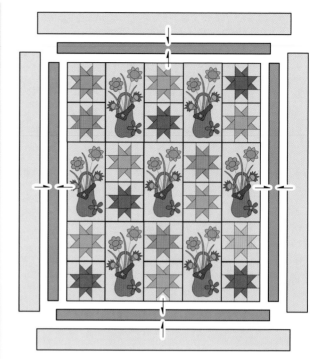

Adding borders

Patterns are reversed for fusible appliqué.

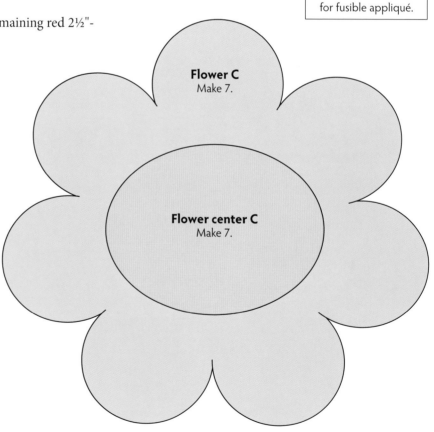

Flower C
Make 7.

Flower center C
Make 7.

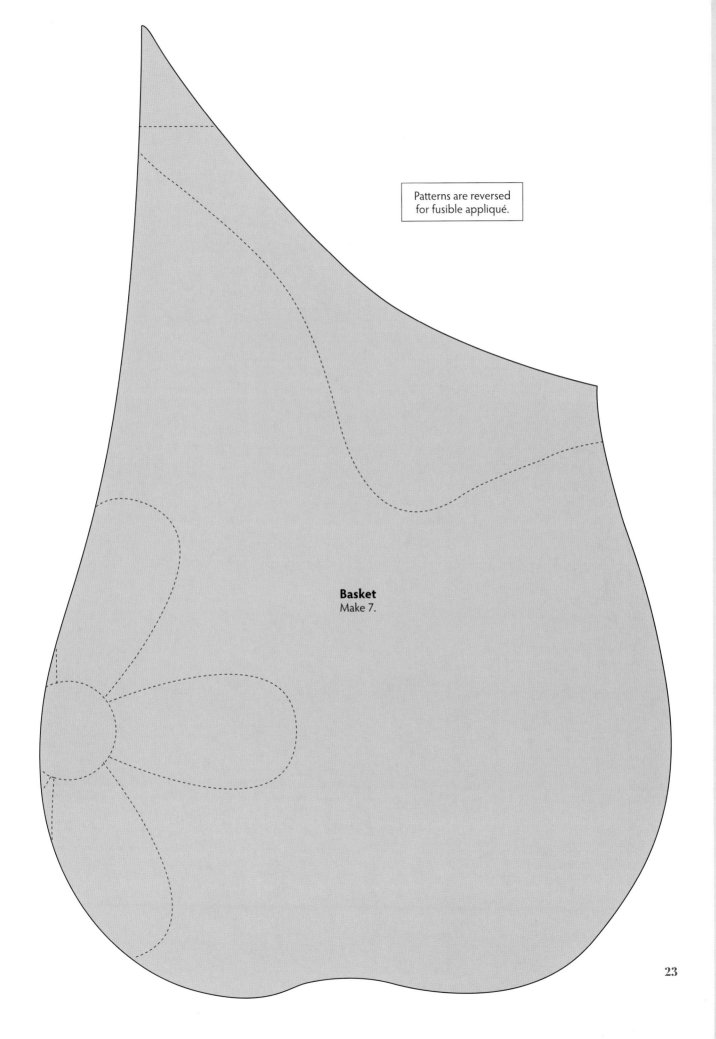

Patterns are reversed
for fusible appliqué.

Basket
Make 7.

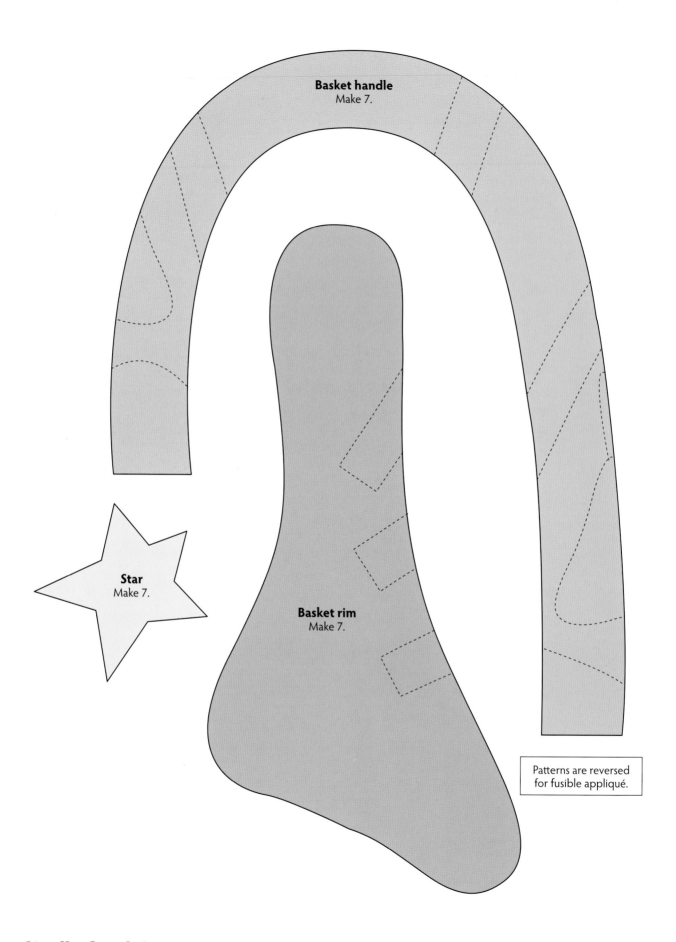

Basket handle
Make 7.

Star
Make 7.

Basket rim
Make 7.

Patterns are reversed
for fusible appliqué.

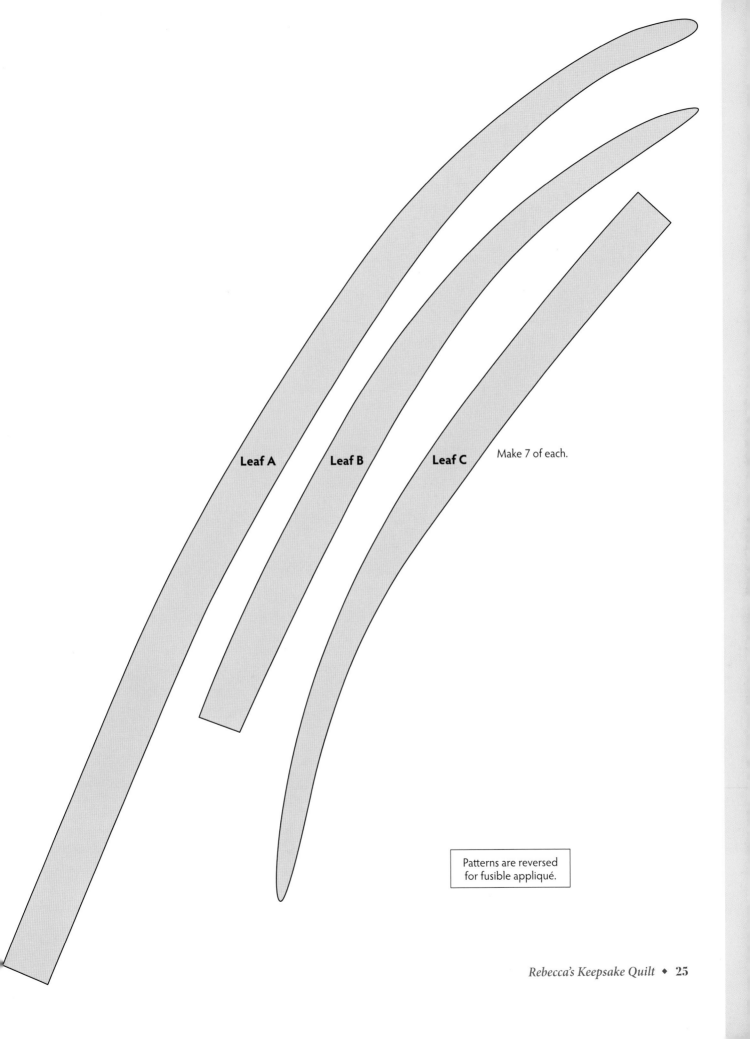

Leaf A   **Leaf B**   **Leaf C**   Make 7 of each.

Patterns are reversed
for fusible appliqué.

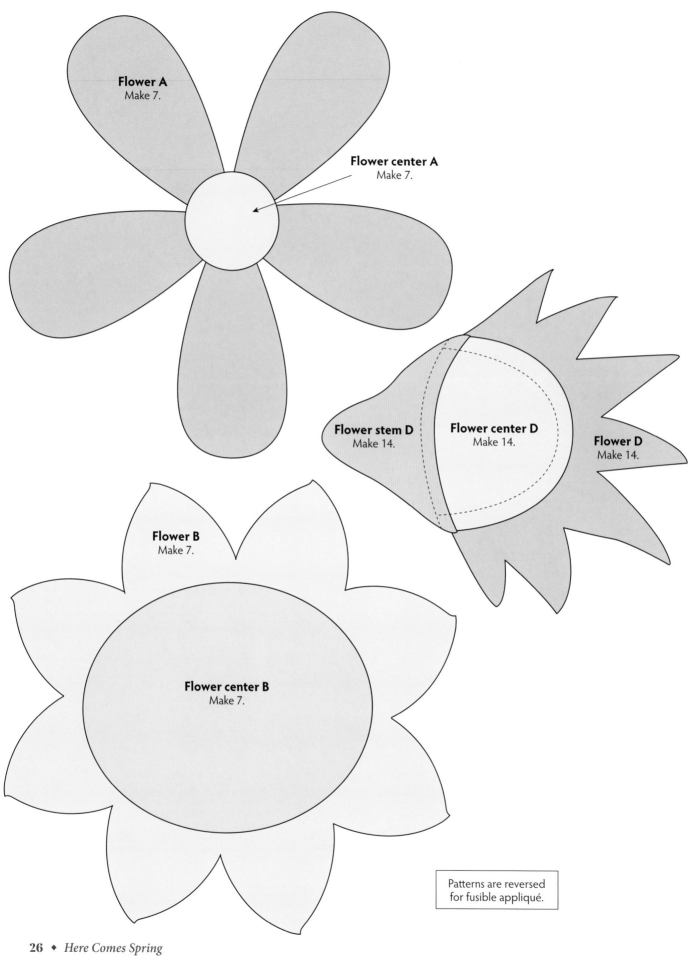

Flower A
Make 7.

Flower center A
Make 7.

Flower stem D
Make 14.

Flower center D
Make 14.

Flower D
Make 14.

Flower B
Make 7.

Flower center B
Make 7.

Patterns are reversed
for fusible appliqué.

Time-Out Lap Quilt

> We all lead very busy lives, and sometimes we need to be reminded to take time out to enjoy our garden, spend time with friends, or make a quilt just for the pleasure of sewing.

Designed by Jeanne Large and Shelley Wicks; machine quilted by Wendy Findlay

FINISHED QUILT: 56½" x 63½"

MATERIALS

Yardage is based on 42"-wide fabric. Fat quarters measure approximately 18" x 21".

2 fat quarters *each* of assorted red, blue, green, and beige prints for blocks

1¼ yards of dark-brown print for sashing, inner border, and binding

⅞ yard of red print for outer border

⅝ yard of light-beige tone on tone for appliqué backgrounds

½ yard of red small-scale print for flowers

1 fat quarter of yellow print for flower centers

1 fat quarter of green print for flower bases and leaves

3⅝ yards of fabric for backing

65" x 72" piece of batting

2 yards of 18"-wide lightweight fusible web

Dark-brown thread for appliqué

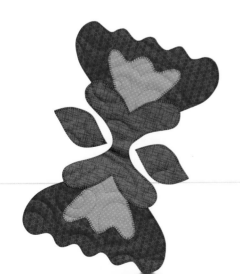

CUTTING

Cut all strips across the width of fabric.

From *each of 3* fat quarters (1 blue, 1 green, and 1 beige), cut:

3 strips, 3½" x 21"; crosscut each color into 6 rectangles, 3½" x 9½" (18 total)

2 strips, 2½" x 21"; crosscut into:
  2 rectangles, 2½" x 7½" (6 total)
  2 rectangles, 2½" x 9½" (6 total)

From *each of 2* fat quarters (1 red and 1 beige), cut:

4 strips, 2½" x 21"; crosscut into:
  2 rectangles, 2½" x 7½" (4 total)
  6 rectangles, 2½" x 9½" (12 total)

From *each of 3* fat quarters (1 red, 1 blue, and 1 green), cut:

3 strips, 4½" x 21"; crosscut each color into 6 rectangles, 4½" x 9½" (18 total)

1 strip, 2½" x 21"; crosscut into 2 rectangles, 2½" x 7½" (6 total)

From the light-beige tone on tone, cut:

2 strips, 8½" x 42"; crosscut into 6 rectangles, 8½" x 12½"

From the dark-brown print, cut:

13 strips, 1½" x 42"; crosscut *2* of the strips into 8 pieces, 1½" x 8½"

7 strips, 2½" x 42"

From the red yardage, cut:

6 strips, 4" x 42"

PIECING

1. To make one block, choose one 2½" x 9½" strip, one 3½" x 9½" strip, and one 4½" x 9½" strip. Sew the strips together and press the seam allowances in one direction. Make a total of 18 blocks that measure 9½" x 9½". Sew the strips together in random order, making sure that you have one of each of the three widths.

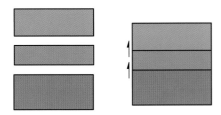

Make 18.

2. Arrange six blocks together into a vertical row. Sew the blocks together and press the seam allowances in one direction. Make three rows.

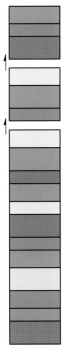

Make 3.

3. Sew together four assorted 2½" x 7½" strips along the long edges to make a block that measures 8½" x 7½". Press all seam allowances in one direction. Make a total of four blocks.

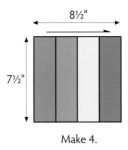

Make 4.

APPLIQUÉ

1. Referring to "Fusible-Web Appliqué" on page 92, use the patterns on page 32 to prepare the following:

   ♦ 12 flowers from red small-scale print
   ♦ 12 flower centers from yellow print
   ♦ 6 flower bases from green print
   ♦ 12 leaves from green print

2. Arrange the flowers, centers, bases, and leaves on a light-beige tone on tone 8½" x 12½" rectangle as shown. Fuse in place. Use dark-brown thread to blanket-stitch around each shape by hand or machine. Make a total of six appliquéd blocks.

Appliqué placement

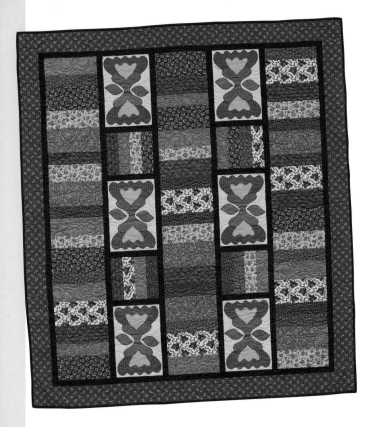

ASSEMBLING THE QUILT TOP

1. Sew a dark-brown 1½" x 8½" sashing piece to each long edge of the pieced 8½" x 7½" blocks. Press the seam allowances toward the sashing.

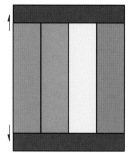

Make 4.

2. Sew the 11 remaining dark-brown 1½" x 42" strips end to end to create one long strip. From this, cut six strips, 1½" x 54½", and two strips, 1½" x 49½".

3. Arrange the appliqué blocks and the blocks from step 1 as shown. Sew the blocks together into a vertical row. Press the seam allowances toward the sashing. Make two rows. Sew the

dark-brown 1½" x 54½" strips to the long edges of each row. Press the seam allowances toward the sashing.

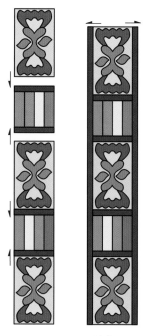

Make 2.

4. Lay out the three pieced rows and the two appliquéd rows. Sew the rows together as shown. Press the seam allowances toward the sashing.

Quilt assembly

5. Sew a dark-brown 1½" x 54½" sashing strip to each side of the quilt. Press the seam allowances toward the sashing. Sew a dark-brown 1½" x 49½" sashing strip to the top and bottom of the quilt. Press the seam allowances toward the sashing.

6. Sew the red 4" x 42" strips end to end to create one long continuous strip. From this, cut four strips, 4" x 56½". Sew two strips to the sides of the quilt. Press the seam allowances toward the red border. Sew the remaining two strips to the top and bottom. Press.

FINISHING THE QUILT

For help with any of the following steps, visit ShopMartingale.com/extras to get free, downloadable instructions.

1. Layer the backing, batting, and quilt top; baste.

2. Quilt as desired. Ours is quilted in an allover design.

3. Bind the quilt using the dark-brown 2½"-wide strips.

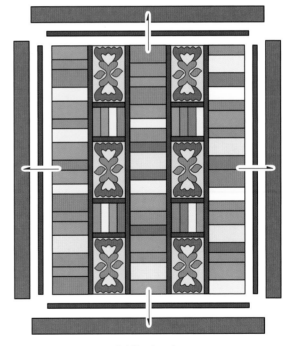

Adding borders

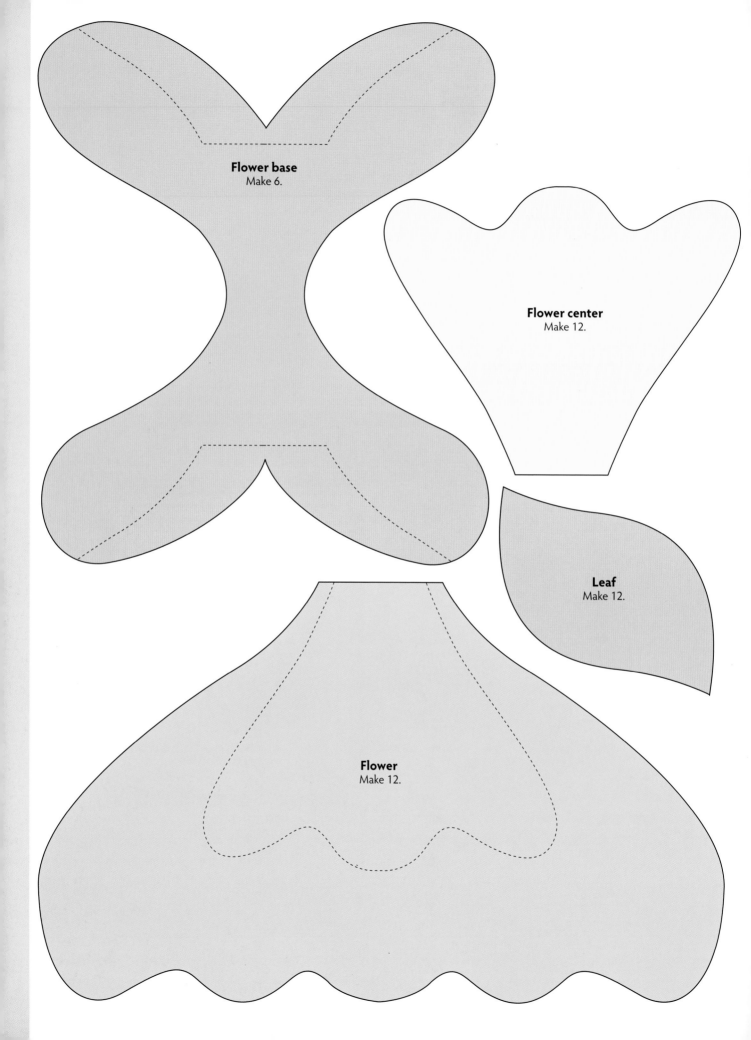

Flower base
Make 6.

Flower center
Make 12.

Leaf
Make 12.

Flower
Make 12.

My Heart Is in the Garden

> Let these hearts and flowers add a bit of romance and a breath of spring to a bedroom or sitting room. The soft neutral background lends itself to any decor.

Designed by Jeanne Large and Shelley Wicks; machine quilted by Wendy Findlay

FINISHED QUILT: 62½" x 73½"

MATERIALS

Yardage is based on 42"-wide fabric. Fat quarters measure approximately 18" x 21".

¼ yard *each* of 16 assorted beige prints for lattice blocks

2⅛ yards of tan print for sashing, inner border, and binding

1⅞ yards of beige print for outer border

1 fat quarter of green fabric for heart D and leaves

11" x 22" piece of red fabric for flower B

10" x 21" piece of pink fabric for heart B

8" x 20" piece *each of 2* assorted red fabrics for flower A

9" x 15" piece *each of 2* assorted red fabrics for heart A

9" x 14" piece of red fabric for heart C

9" x 9" piece of light-green fabric for flower center A

4 yards of fabric for backing

71" x 92" piece of batting

4 yards of ⅝"-wide green rickrack

2¾ yards of 18"-wide lightweight fusible web

Dark-brown thread for appliqué

6" x 6" ruler

CUTTING

Cut all strips across the width of fabric.

From the tan print, cut:

27 strips, 1½" x 42"; crosscut into 80 rectangles, 1½" x 10½"

6 strips, 1½" x 42"

8 strips, 2½" x 42"

From *each* of the quarter-yard beige prints, cut:

1 strip, 6½" x 42"; crosscut into 5 squares, 6½" x 6½" (80 total). Cut each square in half diagonally to yield a total of 160 triangles.

From the beige yardage, cut:

7 strips, 8½" x 42"

PIECING

1. Sew a tan 1½" x 10½" rectangle to the long edge of a beige triangle, centering the triangle as shown. The rectangle will be longer than the edge of the triangle. Press the seam allowances toward the rectangle. Make 80.

Make 80.

2. Sew a matching beige triangle to the opposite side of the tan rectangle, lining up the point of the first triangle with the point of the second as shown. Press the seam allowances toward the rectangle. Make 80.

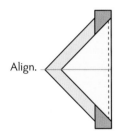

Align.

Make 80.

3. Using a 6" square ruler, match the corner point of the ruler and the center point of the sashing rectangle (½" from the rectangle's edge). Trim the unit on all sides to measure 6" x 6". Trim all 80 units.

½"

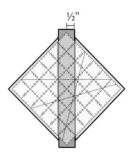

4. Lay out four units to form an X as shown. Sew the units together in pairs. Press the seam allowances open. Sew the two pairs together to make the block. Press the seam allowances open. Make a total of 20 blocks.

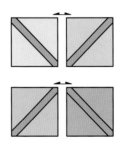 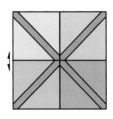

Make 20.

ASSEMBLING THE QUILT TOP

1. Arrange the blocks into five rows of four blocks each. Sew the blocks together into rows. Press the seam allowances open. Sew the rows together and press the seam allowances open.

2. Sew the tan 1½"-wide strips end to end to create one long continuous strip. From this, cut two strips, 1½" x 55½", and two strips 1½" x 46½". Sew the 55½"-long strips to the sides of the

quilt. Press the seam allowances toward the inner border. Sew the 46½"-long strips to the top and bottom of the quilt. Press.

3. Sew the beige 8½" x 42" strips end to end to create one long continuous strip. From this, cut two strips, 8½" x 57½", and two strips, 8½" x 62½". Sew the 57½"-long strips to the sides of the quilt. Press the seam allowances toward the outer border. Sew the 62½"-long strips to the top and bottom of the quilt. Press.

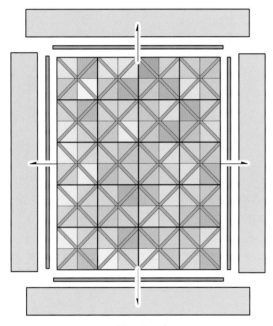

Adding borders

APPLIQUÉ

1. Referring to "Fusible-Web Appliqué" on page 92, use the patterns on pages 37–39 to prepare the following:

   - 3 of flower A from each of 2 red fabrics (6 total)
   - 10 of flower B from red fabric
   - 1 of heart A and 1 of heart A reversed from each of 2 red fabrics (4 total)
   - 8 of heart C and 8 of heart C reversed from red fabric
   - 6 of flower center A from light-green fabric

   - 8 of heart B from pink fabric
   - 18 of heart D from green fabric
   - 8 leaves from green fabric

2. Cut the rickrack into two pieces, 28" long, and two pieces, 38" long. Pin the pieces in place on opposite corners of the quilt top, with the 28"-long piece running along the bottom and top of the quilt. Sew in position with matching thread, referring to "Using Rickrack" on page 95 for instructions.

3. Using the diagram below and the photo on page 35 as guides, arrange the appliqué shapes and fuse in place. Appliqué by hand or machine.

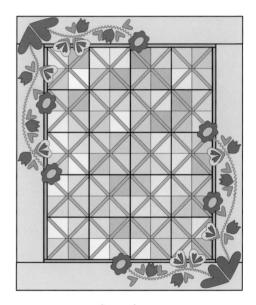

Appliqué placement

FINISHING THE QUILT

For help with any of the following steps, visit ShopMartingale.com/extras to get free, downloadable instructions.

1. Layer the backing, batting, and quilt top; baste.

2. Quilt as desired. Ours is quilted in an allover design with swirls and echoing hearts.

3. Bind the quilt using the tan 2½"-wide strips.

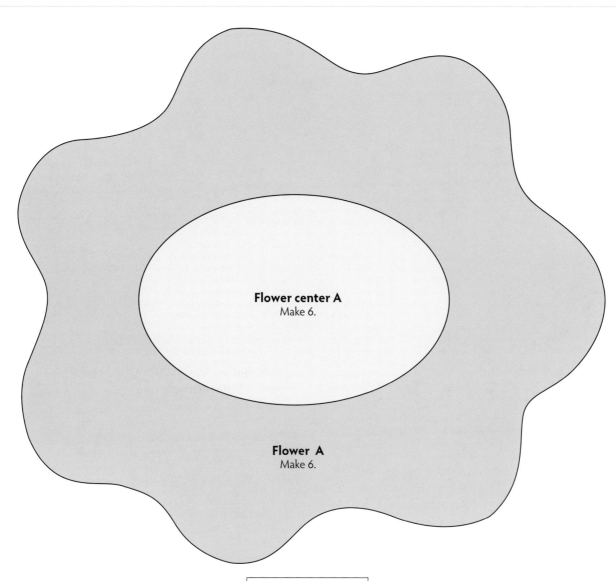

Flower center A
Make 6.

Flower A
Make 6.

Patterns are reversed
for fusible appliqué.

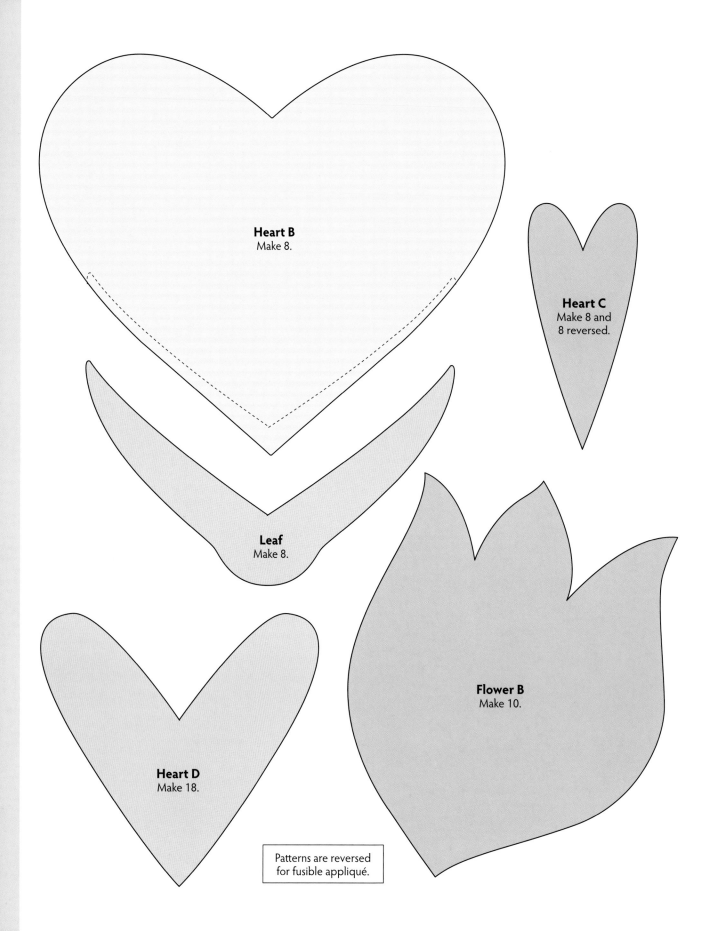

Heart B
Make 8.

Heart C
Make 8 and
8 reversed.

Leaf
Make 8.

Flower B
Make 10.

Heart D
Make 18.

Patterns are reversed
for fusible appliqué.

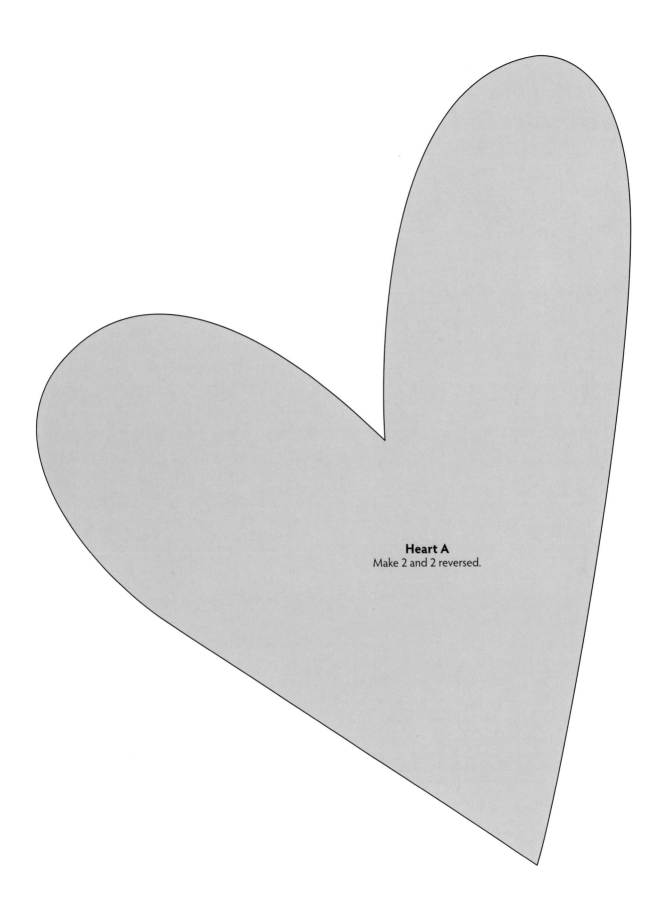

Heart A
Make 2 and 2 reversed.

Plum Pretty Collection

> Stitched in pretty plums and purples, this lap quilt will make any little girl happy! The matching doll quilt and tote bag make it easy to carry essentials on a visit to Grandma's house or when traveling to a playdate.

Plum Pretty Lap Quilt

Designed by Jeanne Large and Shelley Wicks; machine quilted by Wendy Findlay

FINISHED QUILT: 56½" x 75½"

MATERIALS

Yardage is based on 42"-wide fabric. Fat eighths measure approximately 9" x 21".

⅝ yard *each* of green, dark-pink, and dark-purple small-scale prints for blocks

1½ yards of dark-purple print for outer border and binding

⅞ yard of beige small-scale print for blocks

⅞ yard of beige print for appliqué panels

⅝ yard of medium-purple print for sashing and inner border

½ yard of burgundy print for large flowers

1 fat eighth of dark-brown print for flower centers

10" x 18" piece of mauve print for small flowers

8" x 8" piece of green print for circles

4⅔ yards of fabric for backing

65" x 84" piece of batting

1¼ yards of 18"-wide lightweight fusible web

Charcoal thread for appliqué

CUTTING

Cut all strips across the width of fabric.

From *each* of the green, dark-pink, and dark-purple small-scale prints, cut:
7 strips, 2½" x 42" (21 total)

From the beige small-scale print, cut:
7 strips, 3½" x 42"

From the medium-purple print, cut:
8 strips, 2" x 42"

From the beige print, cut:
3 strips, 8½" x 42"

From the dark-purple print, cut:
7 strips, 4½" x 42"
7 strips, 2½" x 42"

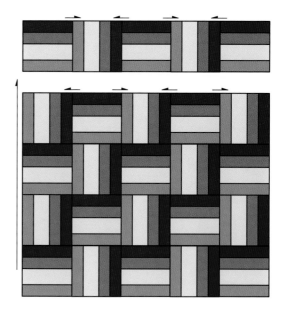

into rows, pressing the seam allowances toward the blocks that have vertical seams. Sew the rows together. Press the seam allowances in one direction.

3. Sew the medium-purple 2" x 42" strips end to end to create one long continuous strip. From this, cut two strips, 2" x 45½", two strips, 2" x 64½", and two strips, 2" x 48½". Sew the 45½"-long strips along the top and bottom of the quilt. Press the seam allowances toward the sashing.

4. Sew the three beige 8½" x 42" strips end to end to create one long continuous strip. From this, cut two strips, 8½" x 45½".

APPLIQUÉ

1. Referring to "Fusible-Web Appliqué" on page 92, use the patterns on page 49 to prepare the following:

   ♦ 6 large flowers from burgundy print

   ♦ 8 small flowers from mauve print

   ♦ 6 large and 8 small flower centers from dark-brown print

   ♦ 16 circles from green print

PIECING

1. Sew a green 2½" x 42" strip, a beige 3½" x 42" strip, a dark-pink 2½" x 42" strip, and a dark-purple 2½" x 42" strip together as shown to make a strip set. Press the seam allowances in one direction. Make a total of seven identical strip sets. Cut the strip sets into 25 segments, 9½" wide, for the blocks.

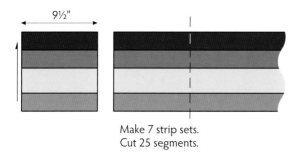

Make 7 strip sets.
Cut 25 segments.

2. Arrange the blocks into five rows with five blocks in each row, rotating the blocks to form the rail fence design as shown. Sew the blocks

2. Using the diagram below and the photo on page 42 as guides, arrange the appliqué shapes on the 8½" x 45½" panels and fuse in place. Appliqué by hand or machine.

Appliqué placement
Make 2.

ASSEMBLING THE QUILT TOP

1. Sew the appliqué panels to the top and bottom of the quilt center as shown. Press the seam allowances toward the sashing.

2. Sew the medium-purple 2" x 64½" inner-border strips to the sides of the quilt. Press the seam allowances toward the inner border. Sew the medium-purple 2" x 48½" strips to the top and bottom of the quilt. Press.

3. Sew the dark-purple 4½" x 42" strips end to end to create one long continuous strip. From this, cut two strips, 4½" x 67½", and two strips, 4½" x 56½". Sew the 67½"-long strips to the sides of the quilt. Press the seam allowances toward the outer border. Sew the 56½"-long strips to the top and bottom of the quilt. Press.

Adding borders

FINISHING THE QUILT

For help with any of the following steps, visit ShopMartingale.com/extras to get free, downloadable instructions.

1. Layer the backing, batting, and quilt top; baste.

2. Quilt as desired. Ours is quilted in an allover design.

3. Bind the quilt using the dark-purple 2½"-wide strips.

Plum Pretty Doll Quilt

Designed by Jeanne Large and Shelley Wicks;
machine quilted by Jeanne Large

FINISHED QUILT: 18½" x 22½"

MATERIALS

Yardage is based on 42"-wide fabric.

½ yard of dark-purple print for blocks, outer
    border, and binding

⅛ yard *each* of dark-pink, beige, and green prints
    for blocks

¼ yard of medium-purple print for sashing and
    inner border

⅛ yard of light-beige print for appliqué panel

5" x 14" piece of mauve print for flowers

3" x 9" piece of dark-brown print for flower centers

¾ yard of fabric for backing

27" x 31" piece of batting

¼ yard of 18"-wide lightweight fusible web

Dark-brown thread for appliqué

CUTTING

Cut all strips across the width of the fabric.

From the dark-purple print, cut:
2 strips, 1½" x 42"
5 strips, 2½" x 42"; crosscut *2* of the strips into
    4 strips, 2½" x 18½"

**From *each* of the dark-pink, beige, and green
prints, cut:**
2 strips, 1½" x 42"

From the medium-purple print, cut:
3 strips, 1½" x 42"; crosscut into:
    1 piece, 1½" x 12½"
    2 pieces, 1½" x 16½"
    2 pieces, 1½" x 14½"

From the light-beige print, cut:
1 strip, 3½" x 42"; crosscut into 1 rectangle,
    3½" x 12½"

PIECING

1. Sew one 1½" x 42" strip each of dark-purple,
    dark-pink, beige, and green together as
    shown to make a strip set. Press all the seam
    allowances in one direction. Make two strip
    sets. Crosscut the strip sets into nine segments,
    4½" wide, for the blocks.

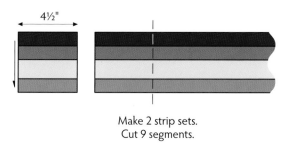

Make 2 strip sets.
Cut 9 segments.

2. Arrange the blocks into three rows, with three
    blocks in each row, rotating the blocks to form
    the rail fence design. Sew the blocks into rows,
    pressing the seam allowances toward the blocks
    with vertical seams. Sew the rows together.
    Press the seam allowances in one direction.

3. Sew the medium-purple 1½" x 12½" piece to the top as shown. Press the seam allowances toward the purple piece.

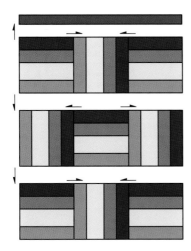

APPLIQUÉ

1. Referring to "Fusible-Web Appliqué" on page 92, use the patterns on page 49 to prepare the following:

- ◆ 3 small flowers from mauve print
- ◆ 3 small flower centers from dark-brown print

2. Using the assembly diagram at right and the photo on page 44 as guides, arrange the appliqué shapes on the beige 3½" x 12½" panel and fuse in place. Appliqué by hand or machine.

ASSEMBLING THE QUILT TOP

1. Sew the appliqué panel to the medium-purple piece. Press the seam allowances toward the medium-purple piece. Sew a medium-purple 16½"-long piece to each side of the quilt. Press the seam allowances toward the inner border. Sew the medium-purple 14½"-long pieces to the top and bottom. Press.

2. Sew a dark-purple 2½" x 18½" strip to each side of the quilt. Press the seam allowances toward the outer border. Sew the 2½" x 18½" dark-purple strips to the top and bottom. Press.

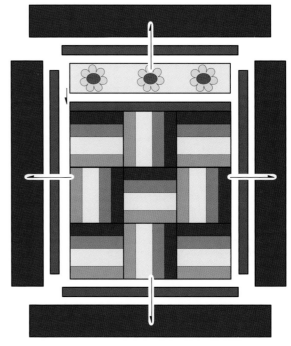

Quilt assembly

FINISHING THE QUILT

For help with any of the following steps, visit ShopMartingale.com/extras to get free, downloadable instructions.

1. Layer the backing, batting, and quilt top; baste.

2. Quilt as desired. Ours is quilted in an allover looping design.

3. Bind the quilt using the remaining dark-purple 2½"-wide strips.

Plum Pretty Doll Tote

Designed y Jeanne Large and Shelley Wicks; machine quilted by Jeanne Large

FINISHED BAG: 9" x 11" x 3"

MATERIALS

Yardage is based on 42"-wide fabric. Fat eighths measure approximately 9" x 21".

⅝ yard of mauve print for bag lining, flowers, and handles

1 fat eighth *each* of dark-purple, pink, beige, and green prints for bag exterior

⅜ yard of medium-purple print for bag top and handles

3" x 5" piece of dark-brown print for flower centers

½ yard of muslin for bag interior*

15" x 18" piece of batting

5" x 12" piece or scraps of lightweight fusible web

Dark-brown thread for appliqué

You can use any light-colored cotton fabric; it won't be seen inside the bag.

CUTTING

Cut all strips across the width of the fabric.

From *each* of the dark-purple, pink, beige, and green fat eighths, cut:

2 strips, 2" x 21" (8 total)

From the medium-purple print, cut:

2 strips, 4½" x 42"; crosscut into:

    2 pieces, 4½" x 12½"

    2 pieces, 4½" x 16½"

From the muslin, cut:

1 rectangle, 15" x 28"

From the mauve yardage, cut:

1 rectangle, 15" x 28"

1 strip, 4½" x 42"; crosscut into 2 pieces, 4½" x 16½"

MAKING THE BAG

1. Sew one 2" x 21" strip each of dark-purple, pink, beige, and green together along the long edges to make a strip set. Press the seam allowances in one direction. Make two strip sets. Sew the strip sets together as shown to make one larger strip set. Press and trim to 12½" x 18½".

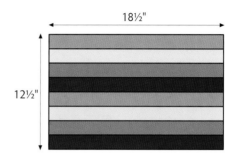

2. Sew a medium-purple 4½" x 12½" piece to each end of the strip set. Press the seam allowances toward the medium-purple piece.

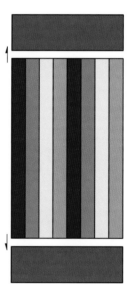

APPLIQUÉ

1. Referring to "Fusible-Web Appliqué" on page 92, use the patterns on page 49 to prepare the following:

   ◆ 2 small flowers from remaining mauve print

   ◆ 2 small flower centers from dark-brown print

2. Using the diagram below and the photo at right as guides, arrange the appliqué shapes on the purple panels, ⅛" from the seamline, and fuse in place. Appliqué by hand or machine.

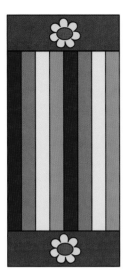

ASSEMBLING THE BAG

1. Layer the 15" x 28" piece of muslin, batting, and bag lining rectangle together. Quilt as desired. Ours is quilted in an allover design. Trim the quilted bag lining to measure 12½" x 26½".

2. Fold the quilted rectangle in half with right sides together so that it measures 12½" x 13¼". Sew the 13¼" sides together using ¼" seam allowance. Press the seam allowances open.

3. To make the gusset in the bottom corners, align the bottom center and side seam. Pinch the corner flat to make a triangle. Using a ruler and pencil, draw a straight line perpendicular to the seam, 1½" in from the corner point. Sew along the line and then trim the corner fabric ¼" from the stitched line as shown. Repeat with the opposite corner.

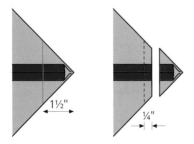

4. Repeat steps 2 and 3 with the bag exterior.

5. Fold down 1" around the top edge of both the bag lining and the exterior, wrong sides together. Press.

6. Turn the exterior bag right side out. With wrong sides together, insert the lining into the bag, matching the seams at the sides of the bag and the edges around the top. Pin the top edges together to hold in place.

MAKING AND ADDING HANDLES

1. Place a medium-purple and mauve 4½" x 16½" piece with right sides together. Sew down each long edge using a ¼" seam allowance. Turn right side out and press flat. Repeat to make a total of two handles.

2. Fold one long edge in toward the center a little more than 1¼" (you will be folding the width of the strip into thirds) and press. Fold the opposite edge over so that it meets the folded edge that you just pressed. Press. Topstitch ⅛" in from each long edge. Repeat with the second handle.

Make 2.

3. Measure 2" from the side seams of the bag and insert the end of the handle so 1" is between the bag and lining. Pin in place. Repeat with the other handle on the opposite side of the bag. Topstitch all around the top of the bag twice, ⅛" and ¼" from the edge.

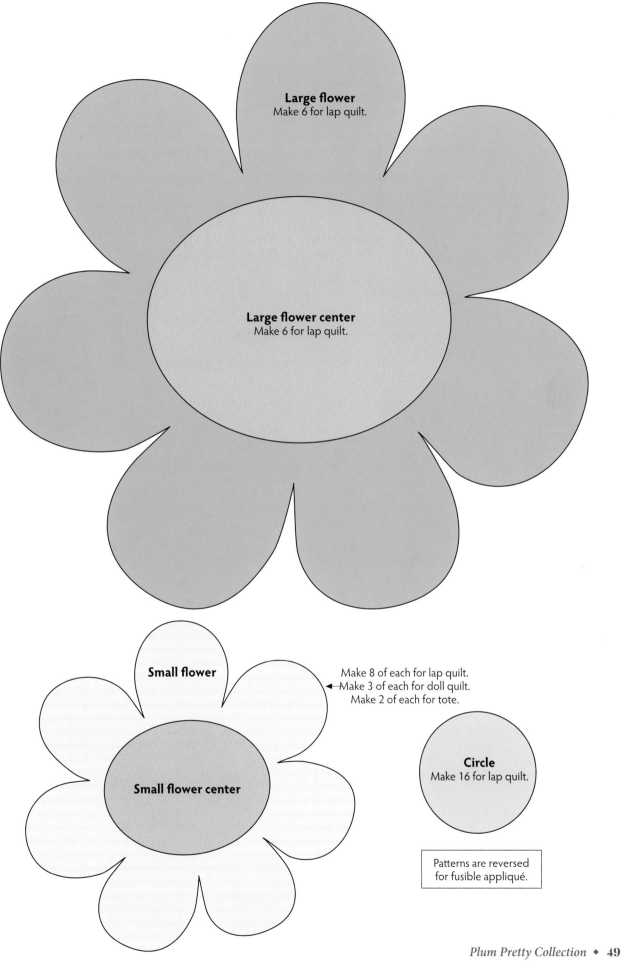

Large flower
Make 6 for lap quilt.

Large flower center
Make 6 for lap quilt.

Small flower

Make 8 of each for lap quilt.
Make 3 of each for doll quilt.
Make 2 of each for tote.

Small flower center

Circle
Make 16 for lap quilt.

Patterns are reversed
for fusible appliqué.

Ziggy Quilt

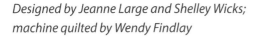

Everyone has that friend who's just a little quirky! So why not make a quilt with just the right amount of attitude and quirkiness for her? Ziggy fits the bill perfectly!

Designed by Jeanne Large and Shelley Wicks; machine quilted by Wendy Findlay

FINISHED QUILT: 60½" x 60½"

MATERIALS

Yardage is based on 42"-wide fabric.

½ yard *each* of 13 assorted red, gold, and green A prints for block backgrounds, circles, and stars

¼ yard *each* of 12 assorted red, gold, and green B prints for blocks

2⅝ yards of black tone on tone for blocks, starbursts, and binding

½ yard of gold print for blocks

4 yards of fabric for backing

69" x 69" piece of batting

4 yards of 18"-wide lightweight fusible web

Black thread and invisible thread for appliqué

¾ yard of 40"-wide lightweight fusible interfacing

CUTTING

Cut all strips across the width of fabric.

From the black tone on tone, cut:

12 strips, 2½" x 42"; crosscut 5 strips into 72 squares, 2½" x 2½"

From the gold print, cut:

5 strips, 2½" x 42"; crosscut into 72 squares, 2½" x 2½"

From *each* of the 12 red, gold, and green B prints, cut:

2 strips, 2½" x 42"; crosscut into:
    4 rectangles, 2½" x 4½" (48 total)
    4 rectangles, 2½" x 8½" (48 total)

From *each* of the 13 red, gold, and green A prints, cut:

1 strip, 12½" x 42"; crosscut into 1 square, 12½" x 12½", and 1 square, 8" x 8"

From the fusible interfacing, cut:

3 strips, 8" x 40"; crosscut into 13 squares, 8" x 8"

PIECING

1. Sew black and gold 2½" squares together in pairs. Press the seam allowances toward the black squares. Make 24. Sew the pairs together to make a four-patch unit. Press the seam allowances to one side. Make 12.

Make 24.   Make 12.

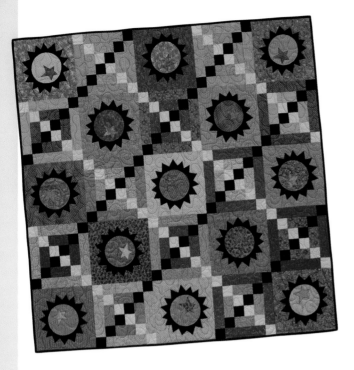

4. Select four matching 2½" x 8½" rectangles. Sew two to the sides of the unit from step 3. Press the seam allowances toward the rectangles.

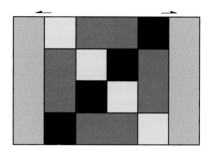

5. Sew a gold 2½" square to one end and a black 2½" square to the other end of each of the two remaining 2½" x 8½" rectangles. Press the seam allowances toward the squares. Sew the rectangle units to the top and bottom of the unit from step 4 as shown. Press the seam allowances toward the units just added.

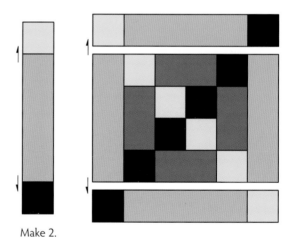

Make 2.

2. Select four matching 2½" x 4½" rectangles. Sew two to the sides of a four-patch unit. Press the seam allowances toward the rectangles.

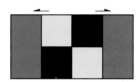

3. Sew a gold 2½" square to one end and a black 2½" square to the other end of each of the two remaining 2½" x 4½" rectangles. Press the seam allowances toward the squares. Sew the rectangle units to the top and bottom of the four-patch unit as shown. Press the seam allowances toward the units just added.

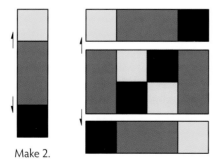

Make 2.

6. Repeat steps 2–5 to make a total of 12 blocks.

APPLIQUÉ

1. Referring to "Fusible-Web Appliqué" on page 92, use the patterns on pages 54–56 to prepare the following:

   - 13 starbursts from black tone on tone
   - 1 star from each red, gold, and green print (13 total)

2. Referring to "Fusible-Interfacing Appliqué" on page 93, use the starburst circle pattern on page 56 to prepare 13 starburst centers from the red, gold, and green 8" squares.

3. Arrange a starburst, a starburst circle, and a star on a 12½" square as shown and fuse in place. Using a blanket stitch and black thread, appliqué the edges of the starburst and the star by hand or machine. Using a blanket stitch and invisible thread, appliqué the edges of the center circle by machine.

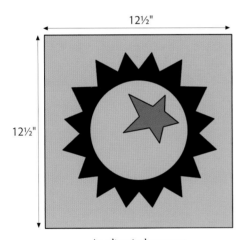

Appliqué placement

ASSEMBLING THE QUILT TOP

Arrange the Starburst blocks and pieced blocks into five rows of five blocks each, alternating the blocks in each row as shown. Sew the blocks together into rows. Press the seam allowances toward the Starburst blocks. Sew the rows together and press the seam allowances in one direction.

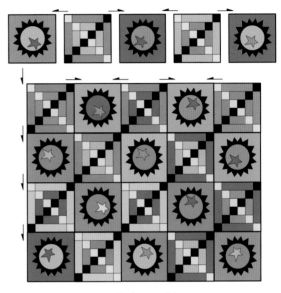

Quilt assembly

FINISHING THE QUILT

For help with any of the following steps, visit ShopMartingale.com/extras to get free, downloadable instructions.

1. Layer the backing, batting, and quilt top; baste.

2. Quilt as desired. Ours is quilted in an allover design.

3. Bind the quilt using the black 2½"-wide strips.

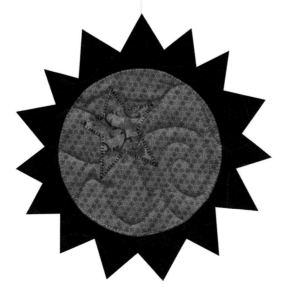

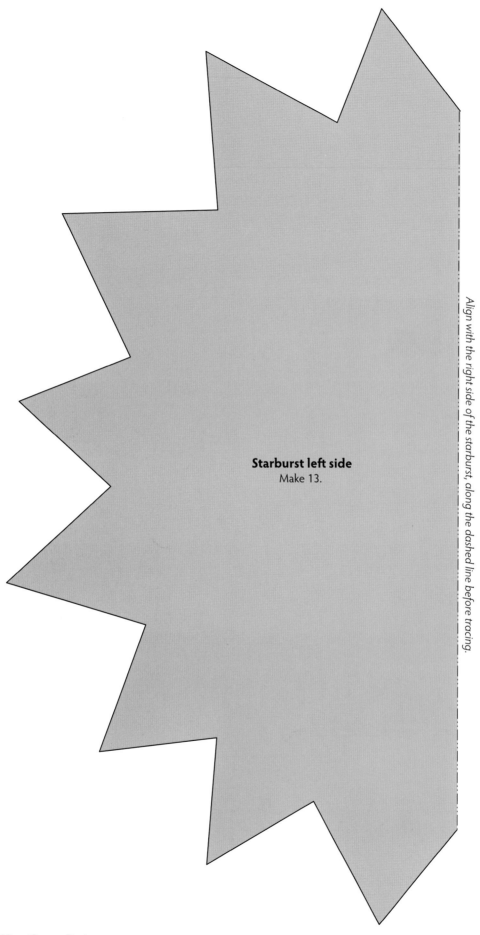

Starburst left side
Make 13.

Align with the right side of the starburst, along the dashed line before tracing.

Align with the left side of the starburst, along the dashed line before tracing.

Starburst right side

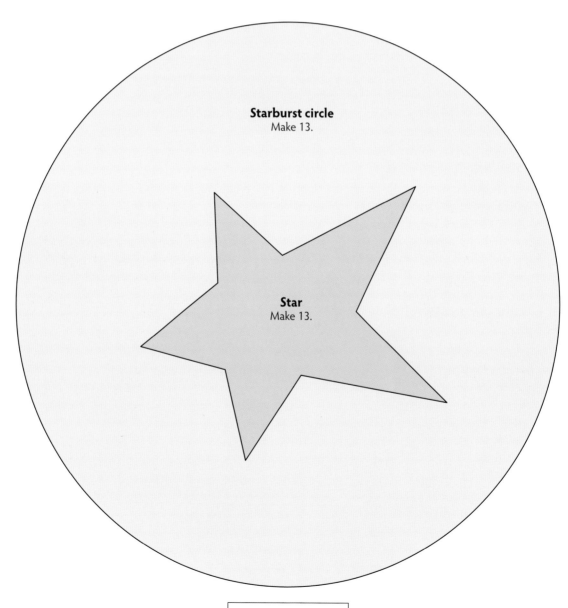

Starburst circle
Make 13.

Star
Make 13.

Patterns are reversed
for fusible appliqué.

Country Cottage Bed Quilt

> Make this quilt as scrappy or controlled as you desire—it really lends itself to using fabrics you have on hand. Either way, it'll brighten any room with its design of stars dancing across the quilt.

Designed by Jeanne Large and Shelley Wicks; machine quilted by Wendy Findlay

FINISHED QUILT: 73½" x 89½"

MATERIALS

Yardage is based on 42"-wide fabric. Fat eighths measure approximately 9" x 21".

¼ yard *each* of 15 assorted prints for Star blocks and Snowball blocks

⅓ yard *each* of 8 assorted beige prints for Snowball blocks

16 fat eighths of assorted beige prints for Star blocks

1¼ yards of dark-brown print for first border and binding

1⅛ yards of beige print for second border

1 yard of red print for third border

7 yards of fabric for backing

82" x 98" piece of batting

CUTTING

Cut all strips across the width of fabric.

From the 15 assorted prints, cut *a total of*:
32 squares, 5¼" x 5¼"
380 squares, 2½" x 2½"

From *each* of the 8 assorted beige prints, cut:
1 strip, 8½" x 42"; crosscut into 4 squares, 8½" x 8½" (32 total; 1 will be extra)

From *each* of the 16 assorted beige-print fat eighths, cut:
3 strips, 2½" x 21"; crosscut into:
    8 squares, 2½" x 2½" (128 total)
    8 rectangles, 2½" x 4½" (128 total)

From the dark-brown print, cut:
7 strips, 2" x 42"
9 strips, 2½" x 42"

From the beige print, cut:
8 strips, 4½" x 42"

From the red print, cut:
8 strips, 3½" x 42"

PIECING THE SNOWBALL BLOCKS

1. Using a pencil and ruler, lightly draw a diagonal line on the wrong side of each of the assorted print 2½" squares.

2. Layer a marked square on one corner of a beige 8½" square as shown, right sides together. Sew from corner to corner on the drawn line. Fold the top corner back and align it with the corner of the square beneath it; press. Trim away the excess layers of fabric beneath the top triangle, leaving ¼" seam allowance. Repeat on each corner of the beige 8½" square to make a Snowball block. Make a total of 31 blocks.

Make 31.

PIECING THE STAR BLOCKS

1. Layer two assorted-print 5¼" squares, right sides together. Using a pencil and ruler, lightly draw a diagonal line on the wrong side of one of the squares. Sew ¼" from the line on each side as shown. Cut along the drawn line to yield 2 half-square-triangle units. Press the seam allowances toward the darker fabric. Repeat to make a total of 32 half-square-triangle units.

Make 32.

2. Layer two of the half-square-triangle units, right sides together, matching the seamlines and laying one seam allowance in each direction. Using a pencil and ruler, lightly draw a diagonal line on the wrong side of one of the squares, intersecting the seamline as shown. Sew ¼" from the line on each side. Cut along the drawn line to yield two quarter-square-triangle units. Press the seam allowances to one side. Repeat to make a total of 32 quarter-square-triangle units.

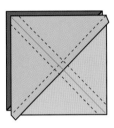 

Make 32.

3. Layer a marked print 2½" square on one end of a beige 2½" x 4½" rectangle as shown, right sides together. Sew from corner to corner on the drawn line. Fold the top corner back and align it with the corner of the rectangle beneath it; press. Trim away the excess layers of fabric beneath the top triangle, leaving ¼" seam allowance. Repeat on the opposite side of the rectangle using a different print. Make four star-point units with matching backgrounds.

Make 4.

ASSEMBLING THE QUILT TOP

1. Arrange the Star blocks and the Snowball blocks into nine rows of seven blocks each, alternating the blocks as shown. Sew the blocks in each row together. Press the seam allowances toward the Snowball blocks. Sew the rows together. Press the seam allowances in one direction.

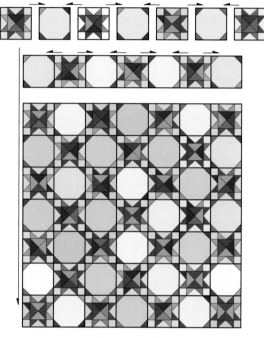

Quilt assembly

4. Sew a star-point unit to the top and bottom of a quarter-square-triangle unit as shown. Press the seam allowances toward the center. Sew matching beige 2½" squares to opposite ends of the remaining two star-point units. Press the seam allowances toward the beige squares. Sew these star-point units to the sides of the center unit. Press the seam allowances toward the star-point units.

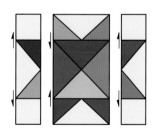 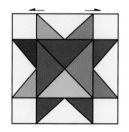

5. Repeat steps 3 and 4 to make a total of 32 Star blocks.

2. Sew the dark-brown 2" x 42" strips end to end to create one long continuous strip. From this, cut two strips, 2" x 72½", and two strips, 2" x 59½". Sew the 72½"-long strips to the sides of the quilt. Press the seam allowances toward the dark-brown border. Sew the 59½"-long strips to the top and bottom of the quilt. Press.

3. Sew the beige 4½" x 42" strips end to end to create one long continuous strip. From this, cut two strips, 4½" x 75½", and two strips, 4½" x 67½". Sew the 75½"-long strips to the sides of the quilt. Press the seam allowances toward the beige border. Sew the 67½"-long strips to the top and bottom of the quilt. Press.

4. Sew the red 3½" x 42" strips end to end to create one long continuous strip. From this, cut two strips, 3½" x 83½", and two strips, 3½" x 73½". Sew the 83½"-long strips to the sides of the quilt. Press the seam allowances toward the red border. Sew the 73½"-long strips to the top and bottom of the quilt. Press.

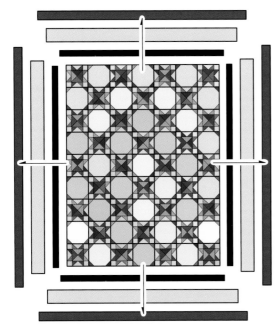

Adding borders

FINISHING THE QUILT

For help with any of the following steps, visit ShopMartingale.com/extras to get free, downloadable instructions.

1. Layer the backing, batting and quilt top; baste.

2. Quilt as desired. Ours is machine quilted with an allover design.

3. Bind the quilt using the dark-brown 2½"-wide strips.

Prairie Picnic Set

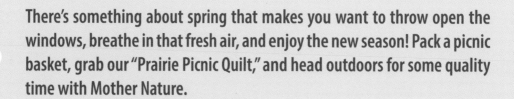

There's something about spring that makes you want to throw open the windows, breathe in that fresh air, and enjoy the new season! Pack a picnic basket, grab our "Prairie Picnic Quilt," and head outdoors for some quality time with Mother Nature.

Prairie Picnic Quilt

Designed by Jeanne Large and Shelley Wicks; machine quilted by Wendy Findlay

FINISHED QUILT: 70½" x 70½"

MATERIALS

Yardage is based on 42"-wide fabric. Fat quarters measure approximately 18" x 21". Fat eighths are approximately 9" x 21".

1¾ yards of dark-brown tone on tone for sashing, outer border, and binding

1½ yards of beige tone on tone for appliqué background

2 fat quarters *each* of assorted red, light-brown, and beige prints for squares

3 fat quarters of assorted green prints for squares

2 fat eighths *each* of assorted red and beige prints for squares

1 fat quarter of gold print for squares

1 fat eighth *each* of green and gold prints for squares

1 fat eighth of brown print for large stars

1 fat eighth of gold print for small stars

12" x 28" piece of red print for flower A

8" x 22" piece of brown print for flower center A

5" x 21" piece of gold print for crown on flower A

5" x 18" piece of dark-red print for inner-flower center A

11" x 22" piece of green print for leaves

10" x 18" piece of dark-red print for flower B

7" x 9" piece of green print for flower center B

10" x 15" piece of red print for flower C

4½ yards of fabric for backing

79" x 79" piece of batting

4½ yards of green ⅝"-wide rickrack for vines

2½ yards 18"-wide lightweight fusible web

Dark-charcoal thread for appliqué

CUTTING

Cut all strips across the width of fabric unless stated otherwise.

From *each* of the red, light-brown, beige, green, and gold fat quarters, cut:
2 strips, 4½" x 21" (20 total)
1 strip, 3½" x 21" (10 total)
1 strip, 2½" x 21" (10 total)

From *each* of 4 fat eighths (1 red, 1 beige, 1 green, and 1 gold), cut:
1 strip, 3½" x 21" (4 total)
1 strip, 2½" x 21" (4 total)

From *each* of 2 fat eighths (1 red and 1 beige), cut:
3 strips, 2½" x 21" (6 total)

From the dark-brown tone on tone, cut:
13 strips, 1½" x 42"; crosscut 8 of the strips into
    2 pieces, 1½" x 16½"
    2 pieces, 1½" x 18½"
    2 pieces, 1½" x 30½"
    2 pieces, 1½" x 32½"
    8 pieces, 1½" x 8½"
15 strips, 2½" x 42"

From the beige tone on tone, cut *on the lengthwise grain:*
4 strips, 8½" x 48½"

PIECING

1. Sew two assorted 2½" x 21" strips together along the long edges to make a strip set. Press the seam allowances to one side. Repeat to make 10 strip sets. Crosscut each strip set into seven segments, 2½" wide, for a total of 70 (6 will be extra).

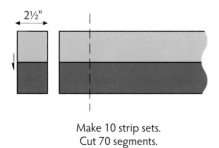

2½"

Make 10 strip sets.
Cut 70 segments.

2. Lay out the segments into eight rows with four segments in each row. Sew the segments together to make rows. Press the seam allowances in opposite directions from row to row. Sew the rows together. Press the seam allowances in one direction. Set aside the extra segments for the border corner blocks.

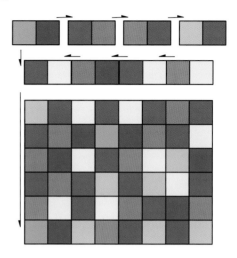

3. Sew the dark-brown 1½" x 16½" sashing strips to the sides of the pieced unit. Press the seam allowances toward the sashing. Sew the 1½" x 18½" dark-brown sashing strips to the top and bottom of the pieced unit. Press.

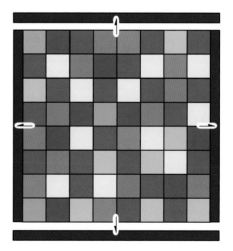

4. Sew two assorted 3½" x 21" strips together along the long edges to make a strip set. Press the seam allowances to one side. Make seven strip sets. Press. Crosscut each strip set into 5 segments, 3½" wide, for a total of 35 (3 will be extra).

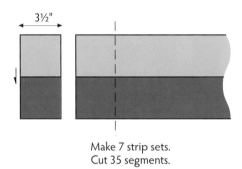

3½"

Make 7 strip sets.
Cut 35 segments.

5. Sew 6 segments together along the 6½" edges. Press the seam allowances in one direction. Repeat to make a total of two sections. Sew 10 segments together along the 6½" edges. Press the seam allowances in one direction. Repeat to make a total of two sections.

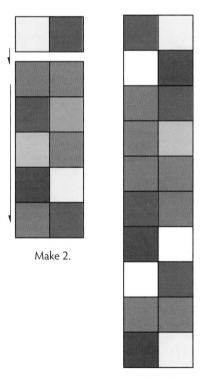

Make 2.

Make 2.

6. Sew the shorter sections to the sides of the quilt. Press the seam allowances toward the sashing. Sew the longer sections to the top and bottom of the quilt. Press.

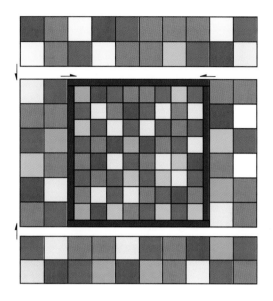

7. Sew the dark-brown 1½" x 30½" sashing strips to the sides of the quilt. Press the seam allowances toward the sashing. Sew the 1½" x 32½" dark-brown sashing strips to the top and bottom of the quilt. Press.

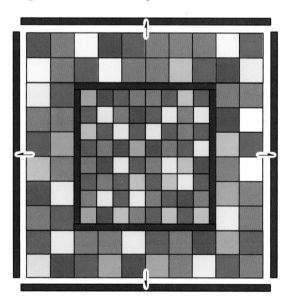

in one direction. Repeat to make a total of two sections. Sew the sections to the top and bottom of the quilt. Press.

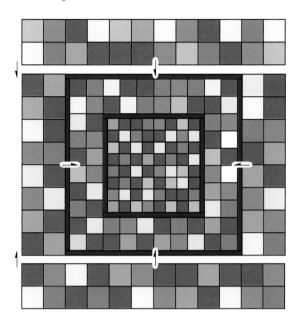

8. Sew two assorted 4½" x 21" strips together along the long edges to make a strip set. Press the seam allowances to one side. Make 10 strip sets. Crosscut each strip set into four segments, 4½" wide, for a total of 40.

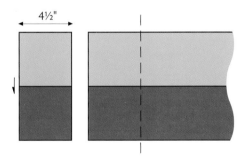

Make 10 strip sets.
Cut 40 segments.

9. Sew eight segments together along the 8½" edges. Press the seam allowances in one direction. Make two sections. Sew the sections to the sides of the quilt. Press the seam allowances toward the sashing. Sew 12 segments together. Press the seam allowances

10. Join the remaining dark-brown 1½" x 42" sashing strips end to end to create one long continuous strip. From this, cut two strips, 1½" x 48½", and two strips, 1½" x 50½". Sew the 48½"-long strips to the sides of the quilt. Press the seam allowances toward the sashing. Sew the 50½"-long strips to the top and bottom of the quilt. Press the seam allowances toward the sashing.

APPLIQUÉ

1. Referring to "Fusible-Web Appliqué" on page 92, use the patterns on pages 73 and 74 to prepare the following:

- 8 of flower A from red print
- 8 of flower C from red print
- 8 of flower center A from brown print
- 4 large stars from brown print
- 8 of inner-flower center A from dark-red print
- 8 of flower B from dark-red print
- 8 left leaves from green print

- ◆ 8 right leaves from green print
- ◆ 8 of flower center B from green print
- ◆ 8 crowns from gold print
- ◆ 12 small stars from gold print

2. Using the diagram as a guide and referring to "Using Rickrack" on page 95, arrange the green rickrack on a beige tone on tone 8½" x 48½" panel and trim. Sew the rickrack using matching thread. Arrange the appliqué shapes and fuse in place. Stitch around each shape using dark-charcoal thread and a blanket stitch, either by hand or machine. Repeat for each beige 8½" x 48½" panel.

Appliqué placement

ASSEMBLING THE QUILT TOP

1. Sew a dark-brown 1½" x 8½" sashing piece to each short end of the appliqué panels. Press the seam allowances toward the sashing.

2. Sew an appliqué panel to each side of the quilt. Press the seam allowances toward the appliqué panels.

3. Arrange eight of the remaining 2½" x 4½" strip set segments into four rows with two segments in each row. Sew the segments into rows, pressing the seam allowances in opposite directions from row to row. Sew the rows together, pressing the seam allowances in one direction. Make four border corner blocks.

Make 4.

4. Sew one block to each end of the remaining appliqué panels. Press the seam allowances toward the sashing. Sew one border section to the top and one to the bottom of the quilt. Press the seam allowances toward the sashing.

5. Sew the dark-brown tone on tone 2½" x 42" strips end to end to create one long continuous strip. From this, cut two strips, 2½" x 66½", and two strips, 2½" x 70½". Sew the 66½"-long strips to the sides of the quilt. Press the seam allowances toward the dark-brown border. Sew the 70½"-long strips to the top and bottom of the quilt. Press.

FINISHING THE QUILT

For help with any of the following steps, visit ShopMartingale.com/extras to get free, downloadable instructions.

1. Layer the backing, batting, and quilt top; baste.

2. Quilt as desired. Ours is quilted in an allover design.

3. Bind the quilt using the remaining dark-brown 2½"-wide strips.

Quilt assembly

Prairie Picnic Tote

Designed by Jeanne Large and Shelley Wicks; machine quilted by Jeanne Large

FINISHED TOTE: 14" x 16" x 4"

MATERIALS

Yardage is based on 42"-wide fabric. Fat eighths measure approximately 9" x 21".

3 fat eighths *each* of assorted red and green prints for bag exterior

⅓ yard *each* of red and green prints for handles

2 fat eighths of assorted beige prints for bag exterior

¼ yard of dark-brown print for bag exterior

1 fat eighth *each* of gold and light-brown print for bag exterior

1⅜ yard of muslin for bag interior*

⅞ yard of 60"-wide natural-cotton duck for bag lining

26" x 46" piece of batting

You can use any light-colored cotton fabric; it won't be seen inside the bag.

CUTTING

Cut all strips across the width of fabric unless stated otherwise.

From *each* of 6 fat eighths (2 green, 2 red, 1 beige, and 1 gold), cut:

1 strip, 3½" x 21"; crosscut each strip into 5 squares, 3½" x 3½" (30 total)

1 strip, 2½" x 21"; crosscut each strip into 6 squares, 2½" x 2½" (36 total)

From *each* of 4 fat eighths (1 green, 1 red, 1 beige, and 1 light-brown), cut:

1 strip, 3½" x 21"; crosscut each strip into 5 squares, 3½" x 3½" (20 total)

From the dark-brown print, cut:

1 strip, 1½" x 42"; crosscut into 2 pieces, 1½" x 18½"

1 strip, 2½" x 42"; crosscut into 2 pieces, 2½" x 18½"

From the muslin, cut *on the lengthwise grain*:

1 rectangle, 26" x 46"

From *each* of the red and green prints, cut:

2 pieces, 4" x 30" (4 total)

From the cotton duck, cut:

1 strip, 18½" x 60"; crosscut into 1 rectangle, 18½" x 38½", and 1 rectangle, 18½" x 16"

1 strip, 4" x 60"; crosscut into 2 pieces, 4" x 30"

PIECING

1. Lay out 48 of the 3½" squares in eight rows, with six squares in each row. (You'll have two extra squares.) Sew the squares into rows. Press the seam allowances in opposite directions from row to row. Sew the rows together; press the seam allowances in one direction.

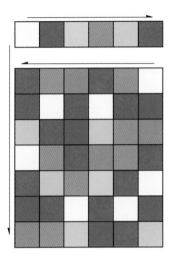

2. Sew a dark-brown 1½" x 18½" sashing piece across each end of the pieced bag exterior. Press the seam allowances toward the sashing.

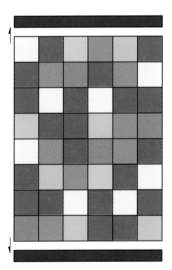

3. Lay the assorted 2½" squares into two rows with nine squares in each row. Sew the squares into rows. Press the seam allowances in opposite directions from row to row. Sew the rows together. Press the seam allowances in one direction. Repeat to make two sections.

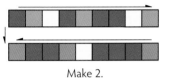

Make 2.

4. Referring to the assembly diagram, sew one section from step 3 to each sashing piece on the bag exterior. Press the seam allowances toward the sashing. Sew a dark-brown 2½" x 18½" sashing piece to each end. Press the seam allowances toward the sashing.

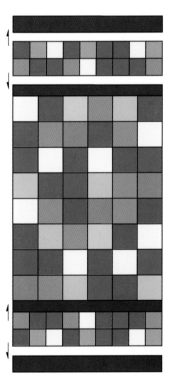

Bag exterior assembly

5. Layer the muslin 26" x 46" rectangle, the batting, and the pieced bag exterior. Baste the layers together and quilt in the ditch along the sashing seamlines. Quilt a crosshatch design through all the squares. Sew along the outer edges ⅛" from the raw edge of the bag exterior. Trim the excess batting and muslin even with the edges of the bag.

MAKING HANDLES

1. Layer a cotton-duck 4" x 30" piece, one red 4" x 30" strip right side up, and one green 4" x 30" strip wrong side up. With edges aligned, sew each long edge through all three layers using ¼" seam allowance to create a tube. Turn the tube so the right sides of the red and green are facing out and the cotton duck is in the center. Press the seams flat along the outer edges. Repeat to make a second handle.

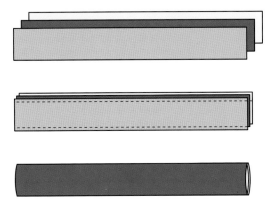

2. Measure 6" from each end of a handle and mark with a pin. Fold the handle in half lengthwise with red facing out. Sew from one 6" mark to the other, ⅛" in from the outer edge, through all layers; backstitch at the beginning and end of the stitching. Repeat to sew ⅛" in along the folded edge. Stitch the second bag handle in the same manner.

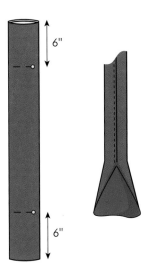

ASSEMBLING THE BAG

1. Fold the exterior bag in half, right sides together and bringing the dark-brown edges together. Sew along each side. Press the seam allowances open. To make the gusset in the bottom corners, align the bottom center with the side seam. Pinch the corner flat to make a triangle. Using a ruler and pencil, draw a straight line perpendicular to the seam, 2" in from the corner point. Sew along the line and then trim the corner fabric ¼" from the stitching line as shown. Repeat on the opposite corner.

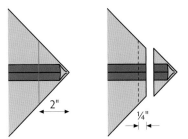

2. Fold the 18½" x 16" piece of cotton duck in half, right sides together, to make a rectangle, 18½" x 8". Sew along the 18½" edge. Turn right side out and press with the seam along one edge.

3. Lay the folded unit across one end of the cotton-duck 18½" x 38½" rectangle, 8" down from one edge. Sew down each side ¼" from the edge and across the bottom to form a pocket. Sew again ⅛" in from the first stitching. Measure and mark a line 9¼" from one side of the pocket. Sew down this line to divide the pocket in half.

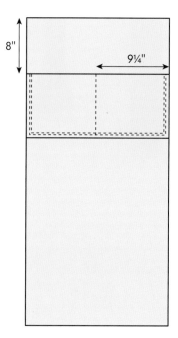

4. Fold the lining in half with the pocket to the inside. Sew down each side and finish the bottom corners as you did with the outer bag. Use a generous ¼" seam allowance so the lining will fit more easily into the outer bag.

5. Fold 1" of the exterior bag to the inside along the top edge. Press. Turn the exterior bag right side out. With wrong sides together, insert the lining into the bag, matching the seams at the sides. Fold the top edge of the lining to the inside to match the top of the bag exterior.

6. Measure 1" from each end of the handle and mark with a pin. Insert the ends of the handle between the bag and lining, 2½" from the side seam, and down to the 1" marked spot. Pin in place. Repeat with the other handle. Pin all around the top of the bag. Topstitch all around the top, ¼" from the edge. Sew again ½" from the edge.

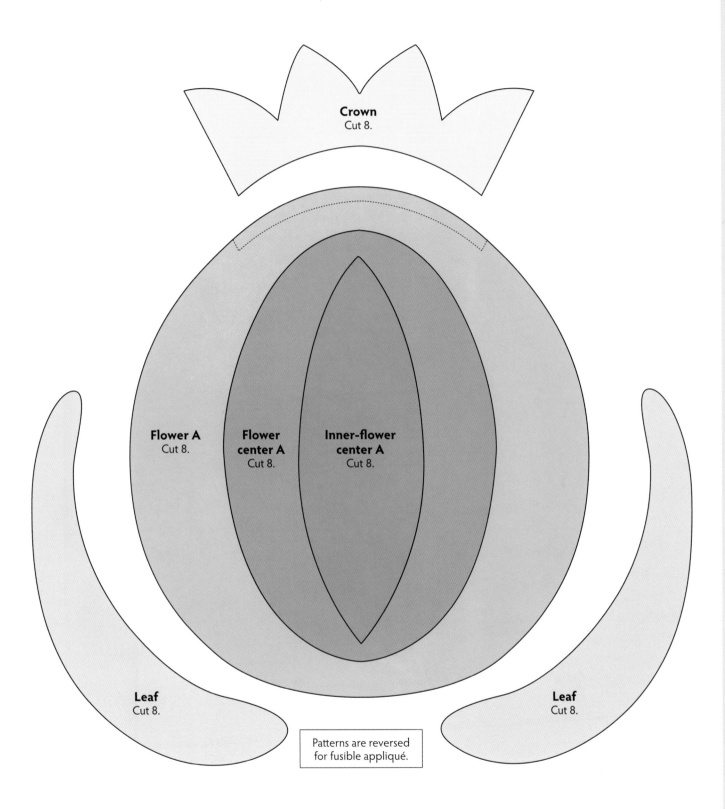

Crown
Cut 8.

Flower A
Cut 8.

Flower center A
Cut 8.

Inner-flower center A
Cut 8.

Leaf
Cut 8.

Leaf
Cut 8.

Patterns are reversed
for fusible appliqué.

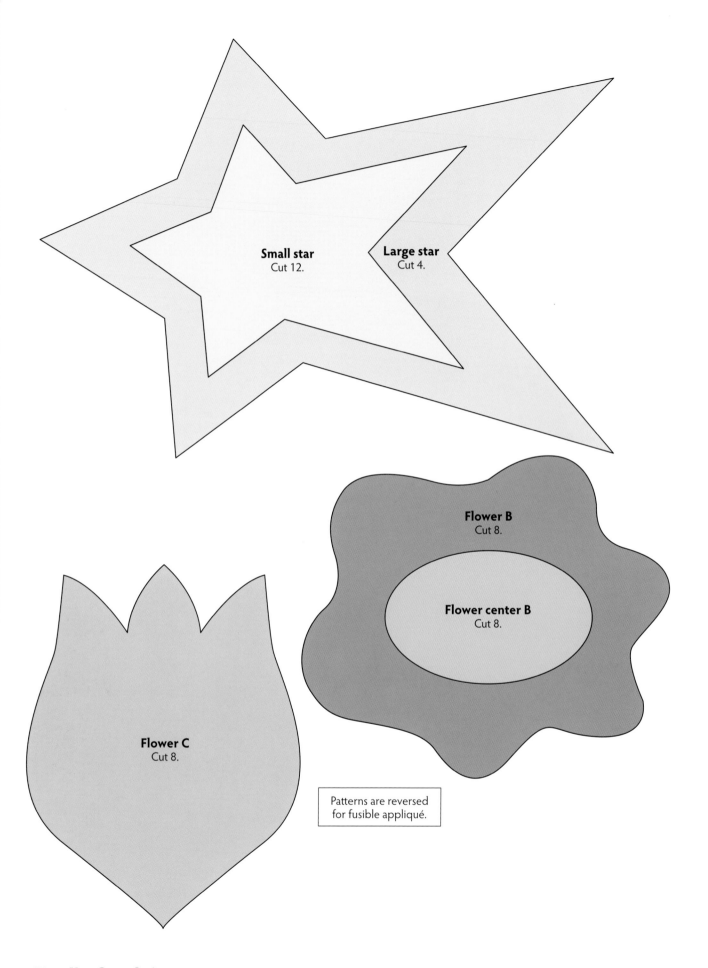

Small star
Cut 12.

Large star
Cut 4.

Flower B
Cut 8.

Flower center B
Cut 8.

Flower C
Cut 8.

Patterns are reversed
for fusible appliqué.

Spring Blooms Duo

> When the snow is gone, prairie gardeners head to their garden sheds to dig out pots, rakes, and seeds to begin a new year. Watching the birds return and seeing those first few green shoots burst through the ground makes every gardener smile. Bring the joyous feeling indoors with this perky wall hanging and table topper.

Spring Blooms Wall Hanging

Designed by Jeanne Large and Shelley Wicks; machine quilted by Wendy Findlay

FINISHED WALL HANGING: 30½" x 54½"

MATERIALS

Yardage is based on 42"-wide fabric. Fat eighths measure approximately 9" x 21".

⅝ yard of red print for inner border and binding

½ yard of beige print for outer border

⅓ yard of dark-brown tone on tone for shed

¼ yard *each* of 5 assorted beige prints for background

10½" x 22½" piece of light-brown print for fence

6" x 11" piece *each* of 2 blue prints for birdhouses

⅛ yard of dark-brown print for birdhouse post

1 fat eighth of white print for window

7" x 12" piece of dark-brown print for birdhouse roofs

3½" x 12½" piece of medium-brown print for shed roof

6" x 12" piece of black print for window frame

10" x 11" piece of burnt-orange print for flowerpot and flowerpot rim

11" x 15" piece of gray print for boots

5" x 8" piece of black solid for boot soles

6" x 8" piece of yellow print for birds

7" x 7" piece *each* of 3 assorted red prints for flower A

3" x 10" piece of green print for flower center A

8" x 11" piece of green print for flower base B

6" x 13" piece *each* of purple print #1 and purple print #2 for flower B

6" x 6" piece of yellow print for flower C

3" x 3" piece of black print for flower center C

6" x 6" piece of green print for leaves

3" x 3" piece of yellow print for boot flower

1½" x 1½" piece of black print for boot-flower center

1¾ yards of fabric for backing

39" x 63" piece of batting

3⅓ yards of 18"-wide lightweight fusible web

2 yards of ⅝"-wide green rickrack

Charcoal thread for appliqué

4 brown buttons, 1" diameter, for birdhouses

CUTTING

Cut all strips across the width of fabric.

From *each* of the assorted beige prints, cut:
1 strip, 6½" x 42"; crosscut into 5 squares, 6½" x 6½" (25 total)

From the dark-brown tone on tone, cut:
2 strips, 2½" x 42"
1 strip, 4½" x 42"; crosscut into 1 piece, 4½" x 19½", and 1 piece, 4½" x 13½"

From the white print, cut:
1 strip, 4½" x 21"; crosscut into 1 piece, 4½" x 10½"

From the red print, cut:
4 strips, 1½" x 42"
5 strips, 2½" x 42"

From the beige print, cut:
5 strips, 2½" x 42"

PIECING

1. Arrange 24 of the beige 6½" squares into eight rows with three squares in each row. Sew the squares into rows. Press the seam allowances in opposite directions from row to row. Sew the rows together; press all seam allowances in one direction.

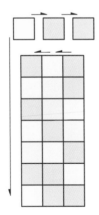

2. Sew the white 4½" x 10½" piece between the brown 4½" x 19½" and 4½" x 13½" pieces. Press the seam allowances toward the brown.

3. Sew the brown 2½" x 42" strips end to end to create one long continuous strip. From this, cut one 2½" x 42½" strip. (If your fabric is wide enough after removing selvages, you do not need to piece strips together.)

4. Sew the brown 2½" x 42½" strip to the left side of the unit from step 2, with the brown 13½" rectangle at the top. Press the seam allowances toward the 2½" strip. Sew the remaining beige 6½" square to the top of this section. Press the seam allowances toward the brown section.

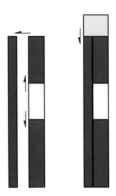

5. Sew the pieced beige background section to the left side of the section from step 4 as shown. Press the seam allowances toward the brown section. Top stitch around the entire perimeter of the beige section, ⅛" from the outer edges. This will secure the seams while you add the appliqué.

APPLIQUÉ

1. To make the fence, fuse a 10" x 22" piece of lightweight fusible web to the wrong side of the light-brown 10½" x 22½" piece. From the fused fabric, cut 6 strips, 1½" x 22". Crosscut into:

   ◆ 4 pieces, 1½" x 20"
   ◆ 1 piece, 1½" x 13"
   ◆ 1 piece, 1½" x 11"

2. Using the 45° line on your ruler, cut two of the 20"-long strips with the angle going one direction, and two strips with the angle going the opposite direction. Cut a 45° angle on each end of the shorter strips.

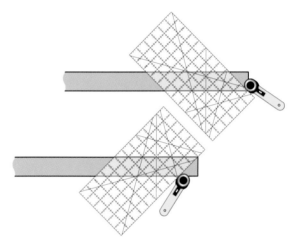

3. To make the birdhouse posts, fuse a 3" x 39" piece of lightweight fusible web to the dark-brown ⅛-yard piece for the posts. From the fused fabric, cut two strips, 1" x 39". Crosscut into:

   ◆ 1 piece, 1" x 35"
   ◆ 1 piece, 1" x 31"

4. To make the shed roof, fuse a 3" x 12" piece of lightweight fusible web to the medium-brown 3½" x 12½" piece for the roof. Trim to 2½" x 11".

5. Position the shed roof so that each edge meets the corners where the shed meets the beige background. This will give an angle to the roof. Trim off the excess that extends beyond the edge of the background and fuse in place.

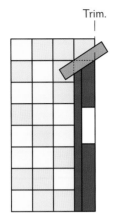

Trim.

6. Referring to "Fusible-Web Appliqué" on page 92, use the patterns on pages 86–91 to prepare the following:

- 1 birdhouse from *each* blue print (2 total)
- 2 birdhouse roofs from dark-brown print
- 1 window frame from black print
- 2 boot soles from black solid
- 1 of flower center C from black print
- 1 boot-flower center from black print
- 1 flowerpot and 1 flowerpot rim from burnt-orange print
- 2 boots from gray print
- 1 bird and 1 bird reversed from yellow print
- 1 of flower C from yellow print
- 1 boot flower from yellow print
- 1 of flower A from *each* red print (3 total)
- 3 of flower center A from green print
- 7 of flower base B from green print
- 3 leaves from green print
- 3 of flower B from purple print #1 and 4 of flower B from purple print #2

7. Position the window frame so that the top, side, and bottom cover the seamlines.

8. Using the diagram below as a guide, arrange the birdhouse posts and fence, and fuse in place. Blanket-stitch around these shapes before adding the rickrack and remaining appliqués.

9. Referring to "Using Rickrack" on page 95, arrange and cut lengths of green rickrack; sew down using matching thread. Arrange the remaining appliqué shapes and fuse in place. Using charcoal thread, blanket-stitch around each shape either by hand or machine.

Appliqué placement

ASSEMBLING THE WALL HANGING

1. Join the red 1½" x 42" strips end to end to create one long continuous strip. From this, cut two strips, 1½" x 48½", and two strips, 1½" x 26½". Sew the 48½"-long strips to the sides of the appliquéd center. Press the seam allowances toward the red border. Sew the 26½"-long strips to the top and bottom. Press.

2. Join the beige 2½" x 42" strips end to end to create one long continuous strip. From this, cut two strips, 2½" x 50½", and two strips, 2½" x 30½". Sew the 50½"-long strips to the sides of the wall hanging. Press the seam allowances toward the beige border. Sew the 30½"-long strips to the top and bottom. Press.

Quilt assembly

FINISHING THE WALL HANGING

For help with any of the following steps, visit ShopMartingale.com/extras to get free, downloadable instructions.

1. Layer the backing, batting, and quilt top; baste.

2. Quilt as desired. Ours is custom quilted with leaves, swirls, and designs that echo the appliqué shapes.

3. Bind the quilt using the remaining dark-brown 2½"-wide strips.

4. Sew two buttons on each of the birdhouses.

Spring Blooms Table Topper

Designed by Jeanne Large and Shelley Wicks; machine quilted by Wendy Findlay

FINISHED TOPPER: 48½" x 48½"

MATERIALS

Yardage is based on 42"-wide fabric. Fat eighths measure approximately 9" x 21".

1 yard of dark-brown tone on tone for inner border, outer border, and binding

¼ yard *each* of 4 light-beige tone on tones for birdhouse panels

¼ yard *each* of 3 light-beige tone on tones for Flower blocks

5 fat eighths of assorted green prints for Nine Patch blocks

4 fat eighths of assorted medium-beige prints for Nine Patch blocks

3 pieces, 13" x 13", of assorted red prints for flower A

3 pieces, 5" x 6", of assorted green prints for flower center A

2 pieces, 11" x 12", of assorted blue prints for birdhouses

1 fat eighth of dark-brown print for birdhouse roofs

4" x 23" piece of dark-brown print for birdhouse posts

5" x 9" piece of black print for birdhouse holes

2 pieces, 7" x 11", of assorted yellow prints for flower B

8" x 11" piece of green print for flower base B

8" x 12" piece of dark-green print for leaves

3¼ yards of fabric for backing

57" x 57" piece of batting

2⅝ yards of 18"-wide lightweight fusible web

2⅞ yards of ⅝"-wide green rickrack

Charcoal thread for appliqué

CUTTING

Cut all strips across the width of the fabric.

From *each* of the green fat eighths, cut:
3 strips, 2½" x 21" (15 total, 2 will be extra)

From *each* of the medium-beige fat eighths, cut:
3 strips, 2½" x 21" (12 total, 1 will be extra)

From *each* of the 3 light-beige tone on tones, cut:
1 strip, 6½" x 42"; crosscut into 4 squares, 6½" x 6½" (12 total)

From *each* of the 4 light-beige tone on tones, cut:
1 strip, 7½" x 42"; crosscut into 1 piece, 7½" x 32½" (4 total)

From the dark-brown tone on tone, cut:
11 strips, 1½" x 42"; crosscut *6 of the strips* into:
    2 strips, 1½" x 30½"
    2 strips, 1½" x 32½"
    4 pieces, 1½" x 6½"
    4 pieces, 1½" x 7½"
6 strips, 2½" x 42"

PIECING

1. Sew a green 2½" x 21" strip to each long edge of a medium-beige 2½" x 21" strip to make a strip set. Press the seam allowances toward the green strips. Make a total of five strip sets. Crosscut 34 segments, 2½" wide.

2½"

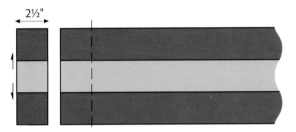

Make 5 strip sets.
Cut 34 segments.

2. Sew a medium-beige 2½" x 21" strip to each long edge of a green 2½" x 21" strip to make a strip set. Press the seam allowances toward the green strip. Make a total of three strip sets. Crosscut 17 segments, 2½" wide.

2½"

Make 3 strip sets.
Cut 17 segments.

3. Sew a segment from step 1 to each side of a segment from step 2 to make a Nine Patch block as shown. Press the seam allowances to one side. Make 17 Nine Patch blocks.

Make 17.

APPLIQUÉ

1. Referring to "Fusible-Web Appliqué" on page 92, use the patterns on pages 88–91 to prepare the following:

   - 12 of flower A from assorted red prints
   - 12 of flower center A from assorted green prints
   - 8 of flower base B from green print
   - 2 birdhouses from *each* assorted blue print (4 total)
   - 4 birdhouse roofs from the dark-brown fat eighth
   - 8 birdhouse holes from black print
   - 4 of flower B from each yellow print (8 total)
   - 8 leaves from dark-green print

2. Arrange one flower A on a light-beige tone on tone 6½" square as shown and fuse in place. Add the flower center. Using a blanket stitch and matching thread, appliqué the edges by hand or machine. Make 12 flower blocks.

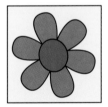

Make 12.

3. To make the birdhouse posts, fuse a 3½" x 22" piece of lightweight fusible web to the 4" x 23" piece of dark-brown fabric. Cut four strips, ¾" x 21", making sure all strips have fusible on them.

4. Using the diagram on page 83 as a guide, position a birdhouse, roof, holes, and post on a 7½" x 32½" light-beige panel. Fuse in place. Blanket-stitch around these shapes before adding the rickrack and remaining shapes.

5. Referring to "Using Rickrack" on page 95, arrange the green rickrack and sew down using matching thread. Arrange the remaining appliqué shapes and fuse in place. Using charcoal thread, blanket-stitch around each shape either by hand or machine.

Appliqué placement

ASSEMBLING THE QUILT

1. Arrange the 13 Nine Patch blocks and the 12 appliquéd Flower blocks into five rows with five blocks in each row, alternating the blocks as shown. Sew the blocks into rows, pressing the seam allowances toward the appliqué blocks. Sew the rows together. Press all seam allowances in one direction.

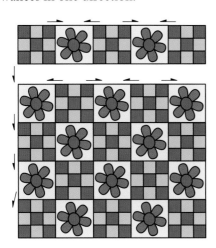

2. Sew the dark-brown 1½" x 30½" strips to the sides of the quilt top. Press the seam allowances toward the inner border. Sew the dark-brown 1½" x 32½" strips to the top and bottom of the quilt. Press.

3. Sew an appliquéd panel to each side of the quilt, reversing the direction of one panel as shown. Press the seam allowances toward the inner border.

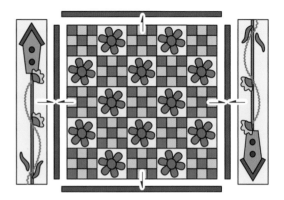

4. Sew a dark-brown 1½" x 6½" piece to one side of a remaining Nine Patch block. Press the seam allowances toward the sashing. Sew a dark-brown 1½" x 7½" piece to an adjoining side. Press. Repeat to make four corner blocks.

5. Sew the brown edge of one block to each end of the remaining appliqué panels, referring to the diagram for correct placement. Press the seam allowances toward the sashing. Sew these border sections to the top and bottom of the quilt. Press.

6. Join the remaining dark-brown 1½" x 42" strips end to end to create one long continuous strip. From this, cut two strips, 1½" x 46½" and two strips, 1½" x 48½". Sew the 46½"-long strips to the sides of the quilt. Press the seam allowances toward the outer border. Sew the 48½"-long strips to the top and bottom of the quilt. Press.

FINISHING THE QUILT

For help with any of the following steps, visit ShopMartingale.com/extras to get free, downloadable instructions.

1. Layer the backing, batting, and quilt top; baste.

2. Quilt as desired. Ours is quilted in an allover design.

3. Bind the quilt using the dark-brown 2½"-wide strips.

Quilt assembly

Window frame
Cut 1 for wall hanging.

Flower pot rim
Cut 1 for wall hanging.

Patterns are reversed
for fusible appliqué.

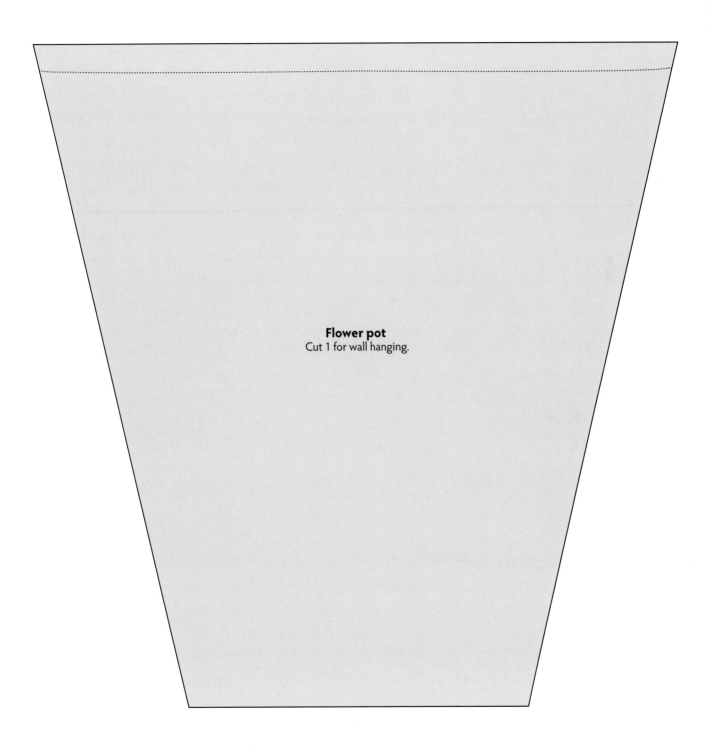

Flower pot
Cut 1 for wall hanging.

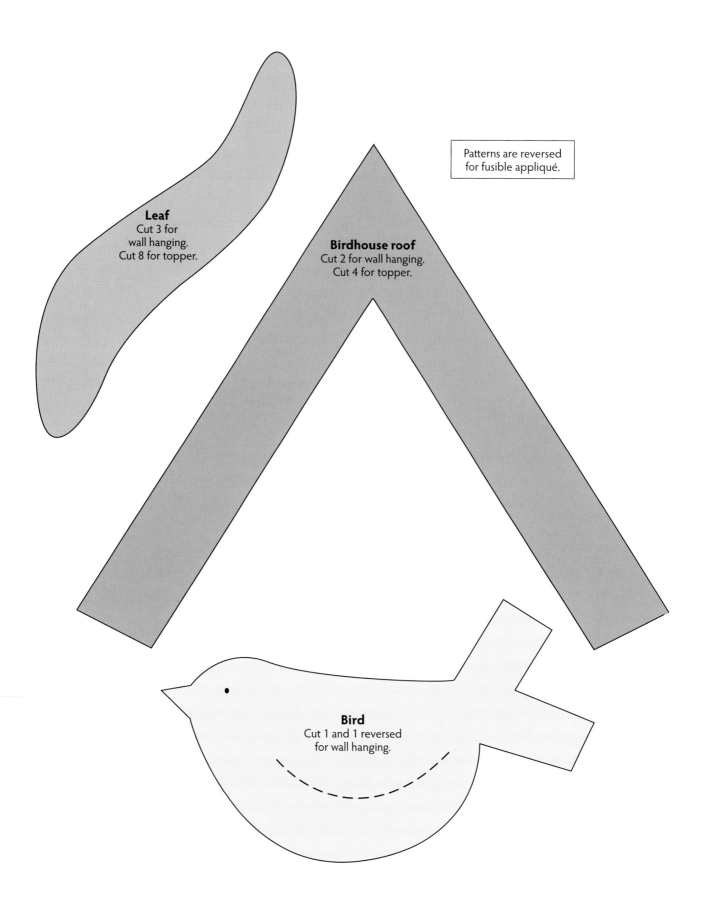

Leaf
Cut 3 for
wall hanging.
Cut 8 for topper.

Patterns are reversed
for fusible appliqué.

Birdhouse roof
Cut 2 for wall hanging.
Cut 4 for topper.

Bird
Cut 1 and 1 reversed
for wall hanging.

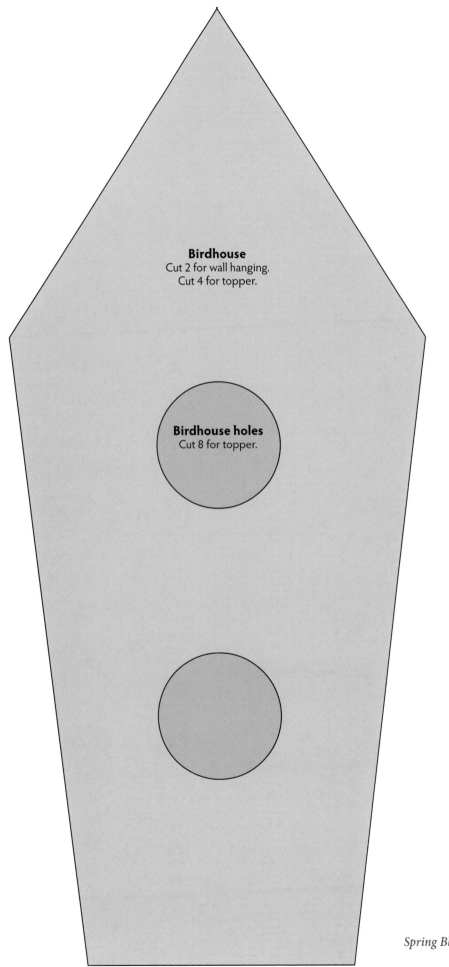

Birdhouse
Cut 2 for wall hanging.
Cut 4 for topper.

Birdhouse holes
Cut 8 for topper.

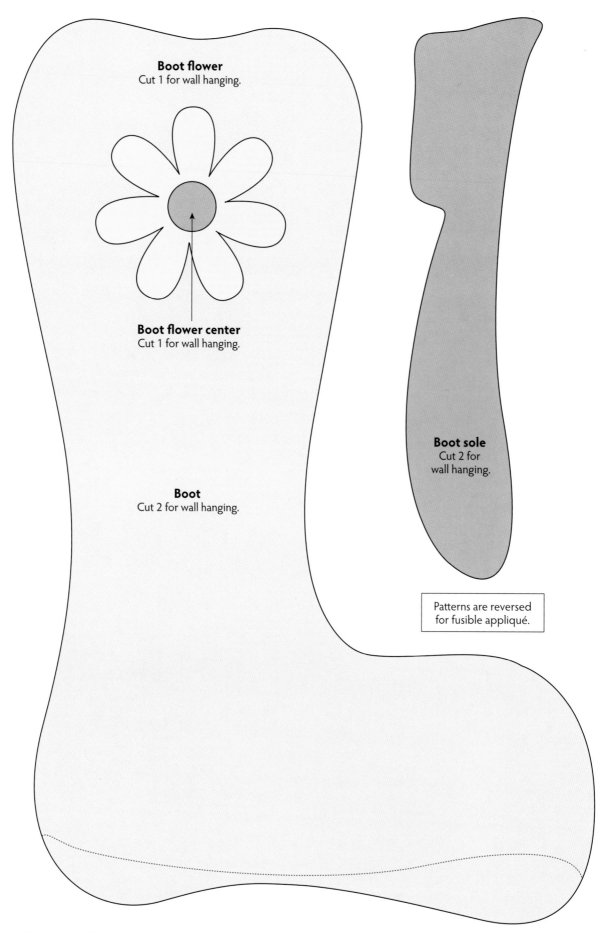

Boot flower
Cut 1 for wall hanging.

Boot flower center
Cut 1 for wall hanging.

Boot
Cut 2 for wall hanging.

Boot sole
Cut 2 for
wall hanging.

Patterns are reversed
for fusible appliqué.

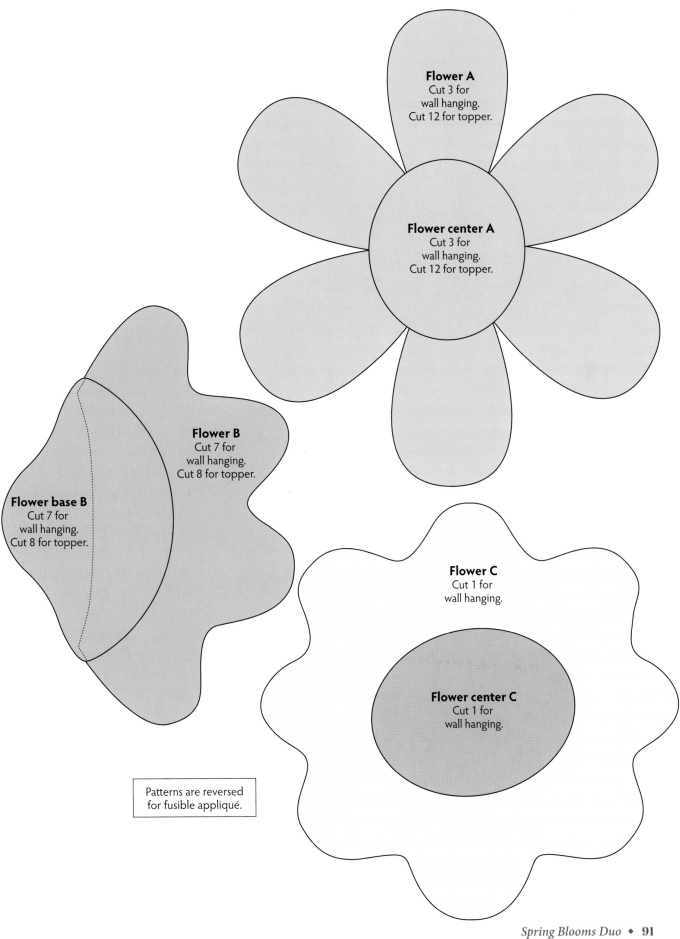

Flower A
Cut 3 for
wall hanging.
Cut 12 for topper.

Flower center A
Cut 3 for
wall hanging.
Cut 12 for topper.

Flower B
Cut 7 for
wall hanging.
Cut 8 for topper.

Flower base B
Cut 7 for
wall hanging.
Cut 8 for topper.

Flower C
Cut 1 for
wall hanging.

Flower center C
Cut 1 for
wall hanging.

Patterns are reversed
for fusible appliqué.

Quiltmaking Techniques

Basic quiltmaking skills are important for the look and quality of your finished product. Most of the time, once you've mastered a basic skill it's yours forever, but sometimes you just want to check to see that you are indeed doing it right. For more help with quiltmaking techniques, download free instructions at ShopMartingale.com/HowtoQuilt.

APPLIQUÉ

Appliqué is what we're all about. Easy, chunky, bold appliqué! Although we love the delicate time-consuming type, we also want a fast, usable quilt. We use both fusible web and fusible interfacing to add appliqué to our projects quickly and easily.

Fusible-Web Appliqué

With so many varieties of fusible web on the market, it's important to find the one that will work best for your project. We highly recommend a lightweight product, no matter which brand you choose. A heavier weight gums up your sewing-machine needle, is harder to sew through, and adds a stiff feeling to your quilts. Be sure to read the instructions that come with the brand you're using. Each product has different guidelines for heat settings and fusing times.

When using fusible web, be aware that any shape that is not symmetrical will need to be reversed. The patterns in this book have all been reversed for you.

1. Use a pencil to trace the appliqué shapes onto the paper side of the fusible product, allowing about ½" all around each shape.

2. Cut the appliqué shapes out of the fusible web, approximately ¼" outside the pencil lines. If the shape is large, cut out the fusible web from the center of each piece, leaving ¼" to ½" inside the pencil line. This helps keep the appliqué pieces soft in the finished quilt.

3. Following the manufacturer's instructions, fuse each shape, traced side up, onto the wrong side of the desired fabric. Press carefully using an up-and-down motion. You don't want your shapes to move around.

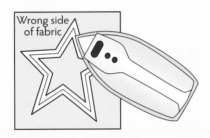

4. Allow the fabrics to cool, and then cut out each appliqué piece directly on the drawn line. Remove the paper backing from each piece.

5. Use your ironing board as a work surface to arrange the shapes onto the background fabric or blocks. Refer to the pattern for proper placement so you can be sure all shapes are tucked under or overlapped where they should be. Fuse the appliqués in place.

6. Sew the raw edges of all the appliqué shapes to the background fabric either by hand or machine. We like to use a blanket stitch. Using a thread color that matches the appliqué pieces will make your stitching almost invisible. Using a dark-charcoal or black thread gives a more primitive look.

Fusible-Interfacing Appliqué

This is a great method to use for large shapes with gentle curves. We don't recommend it for small or intricate appliqué. Before you start a project using fusible interfacing, you may want to test various brands on the market. The fusible interfacing remains in the appliqué, so it's important to use one that is easy to work with but won't make your appliqué feel stiff. We prefer a lightweight woven or nonwoven fusible interfacing.

1. Trace the appliqué shapes onto the paper side of the interfacing using a pencil. As with fusible web, the patterns need to be reversed for tracing, and we've reversed the patterns throughout this book. Leave at least 2" between shapes.

2. Cut the appliqué shapes out of the fusible interfacing, allowing at least 1" outside of the pencil lines.

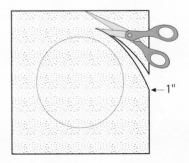

3. Place the fusible side of the interfacing over the right side of the fabric. Pin in place. Sew directly on the drawn line, all around the shape.

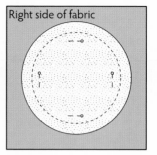

4. Trim around the shape leaving no more than ⅛" for the seam allowance all around. Carefully make a slit in the center of the fusible interfacing, just large enough that you can turn the shape right side out.

5. Turn the shape right side out and gently run your finger or a blunt object around the inside of the shape along the seamline to help ease the edges out. The fusible side of the product is now facing out, and the raw edges are on the inside. Arrange the shape on the background fabric or block, referring to the pattern for proper placement. Gently press the appliqué in place with a hot iron, following the manufacturer's instructions.

6. Stitch the edges down by hand or machine. If your sewing machine has a blind hem stitch as one of its functions, program the stitch so that the point of the "V" just nips into the appliqué. Using this stitch and an invisible thread will

give the look of hand appliqué. Another option is to blanket-stitch by hand or machine.

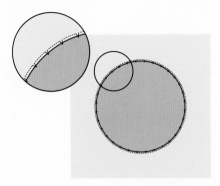

Blind hem stitch

Using Rickrack

Rickrack makes a wonderful vine, flower stem, or accent on a quilt. It comes in a variety of widths and a wide range of colors, so you have plenty of options.

You also have several choices when sewing it to your project. If you're using narrow rickrack, just pin it in place and sew down the center of the strip by machine. It's a good idea to use a walking foot to avoid stretching the rickrack. If you're using wide rickrack, sew the edges down on both sides so they won't roll up or distort in any way when your quilt is washed. Sew the edges using a machine blanket stitch or a straight stitch, or use our favorite method—lower the feed dogs and free motion stitch the edges with matching thread.

Using Rickrack as an Edging

Rickrack is also a great method of appliqué for circles or large shapes with curved edges. It can add texture and dimension to an otherwise flat quilt. Be sure the width of rickrack you choose will curve easily around your shape.

1. Lay the rickrack on the right side of the fabric circle or other shape, lining up one bumpy edge along the outer edge of the circle. Let the two ends of the rickrack overlap slightly and extend off the circle. Pin in place. Using a straight stitch on your machine, sew around the circle through the center of the rickrack, backstitching at the beginning and end.

2. Flip the rickrack so that it extends outside the circle. The raw edges of fabric are now turned under and your circle has rickrack showing all around the edge. Press lightly.

3. Lay the edged circle in place on your quilt. Pin carefully all around the outer edge. Sew the circle down using a straight stitch and a zipper foot. This will allow you to stitch against the edge of the circle without sewing on the circle. The outer part of the rickrack adds a wonderful accent and gives extra texture to your project.

About the Authors

Jeanne, left, and Shelley

JEANNE LARGE and SHELLEY WICKS have owned The Quilt Patch in Moose Jaw, Saskatchewan, Canada, since 2002. Along with the day-to-day running of the quilt shop, these women also design and make almost every quilt that hangs in their shop.

Twice a year, spring and fall, Shelley and Jeanne unveil a brand new collection of projects with that modern country look that appeals to customers of all ages. Their customers enjoy the continuing change of quilts in the shop and know that there will always be something new to see.

With their first book, *'Tis the Season* (Martingale, 2010), Shelley and Jeanne introduced the chunky appliqué, easy piecing, and earth-toned projects that are the basis of their style to

a wider audience. They followed with three more books that continued the look and feel their fans have come to love: *Urban Country Quilts, 'Tis the Autumn Season,* and *Here Comes Winter* (Martingale, 2011, 2013, and 2014 respectively).

Now with this fifth book, quilters can continue to enjoy each project with confidence that it will be something that they can accomplish easily and will look fabulous in their home.

Shelley and Jeanne meet every step of their adventure head-on with passion and energy that fuels the daily workload and fills it with laughter and fun. Both these women love what they do, and it shows in everything they accomplish.

Find out more about Shelley and Jeanne by visiting their website: www.TheQuiltPatch.ca.